HOW TO ATTRACT
GOOD LUCK

ATTRACT GOOD LUCK

Learn How to Control Your Life and Get What You Want

VICTORIA M. GALLAGHER

Printed in the United States of America First Printing, 2019

ISBN 9781794303645

Independently Published
www.VictoriaMGallagher.com

Contents

About Victoria

This book is all about creating more luck in your everyday life - luck with people of the opposite sex, luck with money, and luck for the extraordinary things such as winning the lottery.

Before we get started, let me tell you a little about myself. My name is Victoria Gallagher. I'm a Certified Master Hypnotist, and I've been in business for myself since 1999. I feel lucky in my life, and I believe it really comes down to that in a lot of ways. I feel lucky, therefore I am.

I worked as a stockbroker for six years between 1993 and 1999. For those of you who aren't familiar with what the markets did back then, let me explain. The Dow Jones Industrial Average is a stock market index, based on the values of 30 large publicly owned companies, like Disney, AT&T, and Microsoft. It's a pretty good indication of how the stock market is doing overall. That index rose from 3,300 at the beginning of 1993, to around the 11,000 mark at the point I left the business to start my hypnosis practice in July of 1999. As of the date of this writing, December 19, 2011, the market is around 11,800. It's been as high as the 13,000's and as low as the 7,000's over the span of time since I left the business. All that to say that I was able to work in the field as a stockbroker and could do no wrong while the market continued to rise four-fold during the time I worked in that industry. Now, is that luck or what?

Not only did I get out of a business at what I feel was the perfect time, but I also got into a totally different business then for no other reason other than it was something that I truly loved and wanted to do. It just so happens that hypnosis has significantly grown in popularity over the years since I've been in the field, and we still haven't really scratched the surface of the potential for growth in my industry. I feel I lucked out there, as well.

I would also say that I have certainly beat the odds in the relationship department as I have a husband who is a good-looking guy, a great man, and someone who had all the characteristics I was looking for. People used to think I was nuts when I told them the long list of characteristics I wanted, but they are the ones still looking. I refused to settle and got exactly what I wanted.

Health-wise, while I have had my share of trips to the hospital, I still feel lucky here as well, since I came from a very obese family, yet I have managed to keep my weight in check. At the age of 43, I'm in the best shape of my life.

I could go on and on about my luck. I mention it only because I want you to understand why I feel I have some expertise on the subject.

Funny enough, after I decided to go on to write a book about how to attract good luck, I realized some further validation that makes me the one person you should think about when it comes to luck - and that is my name. You may find it interesting that my maiden name was Gliksman. Essentially, this is a German name, which originates from the root name Gluck, a Yiddish term that means luck or lucky. I was born with a name that translates to lucky man. Then I married a man of Irish descent, whose last name is Gallagher. Of course, we've all heard of the "Luck of the Irish," but, as luck would have it, the name Gallagher means foreign help. I want you to consider me someone who was born lucky and who is here to help you learn how to be lucky too.

It is with a genuine feeling that I believe I have a lucky nature. I simply want to share with you some insights that I have had over the years and help instill within you that same genuine feeling that you, too, can become lucky.

I sincerely do wish you the best of Luck.

Chapter 1: What is Luck?

It is my strong belief that no matter what your background is, no matter where you are standing right now, luck is something that you can create, rather than just having to settle for being an "unlucky" person.

Let me begin by making a basic distinction between luck and opportunity. Opportunity is something that is unpredictable; it's those events that just happen at random in the world.

Opportunity (and we'll use this word synonymously with the word "chance") is anything that happens unpredictably without discernible human intention or observable cause.

Chance encounters, or opportunity, are those things you basically have no control over. For example:

- A job suddenly becoming available.
- A person being at a specific place at a specific time.
- Money lying on the ground.
- The lottery numbers hitting a certain way.

Opportunities are always available, but you have no control over them becoming available. They can, however, turn into a luck situation, depending on the action that is taken or not taken. For example:

- An opportunity is taken, and it turns out to not work out in your favor - one would consider that to be bad luck.

- An opportunity is taken, and it turns out to work in your favor - that would be considered good luck.

- When an opportunity is not taken, and it turns out it would not have worked in your favor, it would be considered good luck.

- When an opportunity is not taken that would have worked in your favor, it would be considered bad luck.

It is how you respond to the opportunities in life that determines your luck. You must take a chance for it to become good luck or bad luck. If you do not bend over and pick up that $100 bill lying on the ground, then you passed up an opportunity for good luck. If you didn't take the opportunity to pick up the phone and ask for an interview for that job which just became available, again, you would have passed up the chance for good luck.

You are exposed to a lot of opportunities. If you don't act upon them, then you are not likely to attract good luck.

For another example, let's say you were at a party. A potential candidate for a relationship ends up being at the party. It could be for friendship, romance, business, or something else. That is an opportunity. How will you respond? Will you decide that this person will not have anything in common with you? Will you rule yourself out as a potential candidate for a relationship with them? Or will you choose to put yourself into a position to meet that person and see what happens? If you do nothing, you may be passing up on something that could be bad luck. But, at the same time you could be passing up on a potential situation for good luck.

At this point, you are potentially thinking that you have a 50/50 chance at good luck or bad luck, and though seems that way, when you act, you are the one in control of your situation. Not only that but acting upon opportunity creates experiences which you can learn from and therefore be able to more easily identify a situation which is going to be lucky or unlucky.

What is luck? Luck is the ability to take the correct action in an opportunity.

If you think that some people are just born lucky, think again. Now, it is true that some people are exposed to more opportunity. The more exposure to opportunity, the more chances you must turn it into luck. On the other hand, some people who are exposed to many more opportunities are not lucky because they do not act. Others are exposed to a lot of opportunities, but they can't see the opportunity that is in front of them.

Still another group of people do see the opportunity in front of them; they desperately would like to act, but they are just not in a position in their life that allows them to grab it. Or at least that is what their mind is telling them. They feel they are lacking in the resources of, say, time or money to act on opportunities.

Yet a whole other group of people do have the resources of time and money, but they refuse to act because of their fear. They are skeptical. It seems too good to be true or that good things like this just don't happen to them, so they choose to do nothing.

In this book, we're going to address these patterns of behavior. Because the fact of the matter is, you already are lucky. You're reading this book, which is a good first step. And when you reach the end of this book, you are going to have created a completely different idea about yourself and the luck you can create. You are going to feel empowered and lucky.

We're going to go over the many different areas you can work on to increase your probability of luck. It's scientific. There are many ways to increase your luck. You are going to learn the exact formula to increase your luck. It's a no-fail system and it will work for you as it has worked for me and countless others.

Chapter 2: A Good Attitude Is Empowering

Attitude is so important. It is probably the most important thing worth talking about in all the self-help material you will come across. Why? Your attitude determines everything you do. It's what makes the difference between a good athlete and a poor one; a successful entrepreneur and a failure; a great artist/musician and one who couldn't carry a tune in a bucket. If you have a bad attitude, you may not wake up as early as you wanted to. You may not go to the gym and work out. You may choose to do the bare minimum at work. You may blow off your diet. You may find yourself disrespecting the very people in your life who could help you get what you want.

What is the secret to attaining the great attitude we talk so much about? Art Linkletter said it this way:

"Things turn out best for the people who make the best out of the way things turn out."

That is the magic formula - nothing more and nothing less.

President Franklin D. Roosevelt campaigned from a wheel chair and won the Presidential election in 1933. He served an unprecedented four terms in office from

1933-1945 as a handicapped person through some of the toughest times our country has ever seen, including the Great Depression and the Second World War. Clearly, this is a man who worked with the opportunities he was given and turned them into luck.

The only disability is a bad attitude. A bad attitude can cause you to come across badly during a job interview, thereby preventing you from getting the job. It can break up marriages. It can drive a person to use drugs or become chemically dependent. A bad attitude can cause a beaten housewife to stay with her brutal husband until he finally beats her to death. It can keep us all imprisoned in our own bonds of self-limitation if we allow it. A bad attitude leads to making bad decisions in life, which leads to nowhere and can make life seem hopeless. Really and truly, after all the lessons we will go through, you will arrive at the same conclusion, when it comes to changing your luck, it begins and ends with changing your attitude.

Attitude is not the only component, but it's an essential part of the formula to change your luck because your attitude is the foundation from which everything else you do in the endeavor of learning how to become luckier will begin. Without this part of the equation, you simply cannot be lucky.

Henry Ford said:

"Whether you think that you can, or that you can't, you are usually right."

Whatever hand of cards you were dealt, you must realize that you have the capacity to change your luck and change your life into whatever you want it to be.

You could greet each day with a positive attitude and watch the difference it makes. Someone once said that life is 10% what happens to you and 90% how you deal with it. That is why having a good attitude is so important. It empowers you, and when you are empowered, you can empower everyone else you encounter.

Today, give it a try and put on that mask of a good attitude. Yes, that's right, sometimes you will have to "fake it till you make it", but in the long run you will see that having a good attitude will get easier and easier until it becomes second nature to you. Today, be empowered and decide to face your day with a good attitude!

Chapter 3: How to Align Your Mind with Luck.

The first thing to establish before we go further is to get the support of your subconscious mind. And the most efficient and effective way to accomplish that is to change your thought patterns when it comes to luck.

Do you ever find yourself saying things like this?

"I have the worst luck in the world."

"Everyone else is lucky, but not me."

"Why does this ALWAYS happen to me?"

These are direct suggestions to your subconscious mind. Whether you think you are saying something in a lighthearted way or you are very passionate when you say it, you are giving your subconscious mind a direct command to carry out the reality that, "I have the worst luck in the world."

You are programming yourself to receive even more bad luck in the future. Since you think you are an unlucky person, your subconscious mind believes that and whatever your subconscious mind believes, it must carry that out to fruition. That's its job.

What does it look like for your subconscious mind to carry out the command? It looks like avoiding a lot of opportunities that could have been lucky for you, if given the chance. Your subconscious mind looks for and sets up circumstances to make your belief correct about the fact that you are unlucky. You even feel justified about your bad luck because you can now look back on that opportunity you passed up and say, "See how unlucky I was?"

People love being right about how bad it is for them so much so that they may even find themselves in a bragging war, boasting about just how unlucky they have been or just how big of a victim they are in life. Haven't you ever noticed just how much people love to talk about how bad they have it? Now, let's be honest.

Do you ever find yourself making any of these types of statements?

"They keep doing it to me."

"If it weren't for (X), I'd be happy, make more money, feel better, etc."

"Why do bad things keep happening to me?

"You made me mad"

"I couldn't do that because ..."

These are called "victim statements," and they are basically placing the blame on someone or something else for what happens to you. Someone else is to blame. If it weren't for this or that, then you'd have a better situation.

The problem with this way of thinking is that it is very disempowering. You believe that other people or events or things have the control and can prevent you from having what you want. And when you have this belief, you struggle to succeed in life because of all these obstacles that you feel you have no control over.

If you are struggling to attract good luck in your life, then it may be because you have been playing the role of the victim. You've been indulging in too much pity-partying and feeling sorry for yourself, or you've been mad at those who are holding you back. You've convinced yourself that you're just one of those unfortunate people who have bad luck. You've pleaded your case to your friends and family members, defending all the obstacles standing in your way and how these obstacles prevent you from ever getting a lucky break.

What if I told you that these obstacles are just your own illusions? These obstacles are not real. Oh, they seem very real. But they are only real in your imagination. Your imagination makes things seem very real.

We've been brainwashed since birth to believe:

"I'm not worthy"

"There's not enough to go around"

"You'll never amount to much"

"I'm not good enough"

These deep-seated beliefs are so ingrained within your subconscious mind, you don't even realize they are there. But they creep into every corner of your life and take away your power to create the life you really want.

These messages aren't necessarily told to you verbally, though. Perhaps, at some very early, long-forgotten stage of your life, you accepted these ideas as facts as you watched your parents struggle to survive. It's so much easier to believe in a negative world because that's all we see and hear all around us.

Maybe you have experienced failure after failure, broken promises, and goals never realized. How could you believe anything other than that you are unlucky, and things just "happen" to you, and you have no control over it? Is this a reality you would have accepted had you been given the choice?

Coming into our human experience, we tend to think we came here to suffer and deal with all sorts of dilemmas. Sometimes we really torture ourselves with this illusion of powerlessness and forget who we really are at the deepest level.

While the challenges we have set up for ourselves help us to learn from our human life experiences, consider the idea that the reality in your mind is not the one and only true reality. It's a reality that you have been developing since birth, based on everything you've ever heard, seen, or experienced in any conceivable way. These experiences have created what is called your belief system, or your filters.

Since your beliefs are buried deep in your subconscious, your life is just one cycle of beliefs creating experiences, and your experiences reinforcing your beliefs.

Consider this: who you believe you are is not who you really are. Who you really are is much more powerful than you may comprehend right now.

What if you are one of the lucky ones?

Imagine for a moment that you are the source of complete and total power, and you determine the course of your own life. What if you could accomplish great things like Einstein, Beethoven, and Thomas Edison? What if you really knew that you do have the power to acquire wealth, health, love, and just about anything else you can dream up?

Then ask, "Why can't I be someone like that?"

You can choose, at any moment, to change your story about luck. Wouldn't now be a good time to change that story?

I'm hearing a big resounding, "Yes!"

"What about the Victim?"

At least, the consciously aware part of you is saying, "Yes!" But what about the part of you that still likes to be a victim? Does that part of you want to change the story too? Or does it still want to keep moaning and groaning about how bad it is?

Before you answer that question, let's gain some more insight into what the victim is getting out of all the moaning and groaning.

As human beings, we are motivated by benefits. We simply do not do anything unless there is a benefit involved. I know that seems selfish of us all, but it's true. No matter what you are doing, whether it's bad or good, wrong or right, being lazy or motivated, being angry or happy, working or playing, whatever it is, you are motivated by pleasure or pain.

At the root of every behavior is a need to move toward pleasure or move away from pain. Stated another way, there's an underlying positive intention for everything we do.

This does not imply that everything you do has a positive result. What it means is that actions and behaviors have a positive intention. It is done to obtain an unconscious desired goal. And that goal is either to make you feel good or make you stop feeling bad.

The victim part of you is doing what it does with good intention. It has a positive motive. It wants you to feel good, or it wants you to stop feeling bad.

Isn't that nice? It is nice. It's just that the approach; i.e. being a victim, might be holding you back from having what you really want.

Now, this is where you get a chance to really take the first step toward changing your luck. And while it may be the first step, it's the hardest one of them all for some people. It doesn't have to be, though. The more honest and sincerer you are with yourself right now, the more quickly and easily you can change.

You see, this part of the process of changing your luck is like building a card house. It's like building any kind of house or structure, for that matter. What do you need in order to build a new structure, which will provide long-lasting dependability and stability?

You need to start with a good, solid foundation. The victim, while well intentioned, is a weak link in your foundation and it can undermine your efforts to change your luck. You cannot really change your luck if some unaware part of yourself feels powerless to change your life.

You want to build a structure that is unshakeable and that is totally aligned from top to bottom with your beliefs, desires, and everything in between. You want a durable structure that can weather any storm and remain strong.

Before you can be strong however, you must begin by being vulnerable. The more open and honest you can be right now, the better this is going to work and the stronger the foundation you will have to build upon.

Vulnerability sometimes gets a bad rap. It's a very misunderstood term. In a nutshell though, strength and vulnerability are two opposites.

In this world of duality and yin and yang, you need both to appreciate both. To be stronger, you must become more vulnerable. To be vulnerable requires some inner strength.

One can't really know happiness without knowing sadness. Don't confuse the word vulnerability with weakness. It takes strength to do this work of exposing and acknowledging what it is about you that needs to change.

Are you up for the challenge? Good, I thought you would say yes!

Here are the steps you will take:

- The first step is Awareness of the behavior you want to change. It's important for you to realize, though, that you are not your behavior.

- The second step is to understand the Motivation behind the behavior.

- The third step is you must Want to change. Why are you motivated to change your behavior (let's call it your attitude)? You want to change your attitude because your attitude is in direct correlation with the amount of luck you have in your life. The better your attitude is, the more luck you are going to have. Of course, there are more resources than just your attitude, but it all starts there.

- The fourth step is to Replace the old behavior with a new behavior. The old behavior was filling a need of some sort as identified in step two. You cannot just stop doing something and leave an empty hole where something once was. You still have the need. By default, the hole will fill up with something else. Most likely the old behavior will just come back. Or it might be replaced by an even worse behavior.

When you pull up a weed from the ground, another weed is going to grow in its place. It's not going to suddenly start growing a rose bush, unless you plant rosebuds. In this step you will come up with the new behavior to fulfill that need.

- The fifth step is to Integrate the change into your subconscious mind.

Step 1: Awareness

Let's identify that behavior. You can call it whatever you want - victim mentality, attitude, or negative thinking.

Start by finishing the following statement with one or two words having to do with the behavior you would like to change:

The reason I have had issues with attracting good luck is:

_____

(i.e., my victim mentality, my negative thinking, my attitude)

Step 2: Understand the Motivation:

Some of the potential motivations you may possess from having a victim mentality are as follows:

Attention and validation. You seem to get good feelings from other people when they are concerned about you and try to help you out. On the other hand, it may not last very long as people get tired of constantly validating you.

You don't have to take risks. When you feel like a victim, you tend to not act, and then you don't have to risk, for example, rejection or failure.

You don't have to take the sometimes-heavy responsibility. Taking responsibility for your own life can be hard work - you must make difficult decisions, and it gets heavy sometimes. In the short term, it can feel like the easier choice to not take personal responsibility.

It makes you feel right. When you feel like the victim and like everyone else is wrong and you are right, then that can lead to pleasurable feelings.

Do you identify with any of those benefits?

Get in touch with the benefits you have been getting out of having this sort of attitude about your luck. What is the positive intention you get from this behavior (i.e., having this attitude, negative thinking, or victim mentality)?

_____

I have been behaving with a: (Insert Answer from Step #1)

_____

because of my need for: (What is the need, the motivation, the benefit you are getting? Insert Answer from Step #2)

_____

Step 3: Do you want to change your behavior and why?

Now that you realize you have this behavior, and you know what you get from the behavior, the question is simple: do you want to change and why?

Do you want to change?

Yes or No

(just circle one)

Why? What would be the benefit of changing? Write a sentence or two about why you want to change.

I want to change this behavior because:

_____

_____

_____

Step 4: Replace the old behavior

I have been behaving with a (Answer from Step #1):

_____

because of my need for (What is the need, the motivation, the benefit you are getting?):

I want to change this behavior because (answer from Step #3):

I want to change this behavior because:

_____

_____

_____

and instead of behaving with a (Answer from Step #1):

_____

I choose to replace that old behavior with this new behavior (Choose new positive behavior):

_____

Step 5: Subconscious Integration:

We are going to do an NLP (Neuro-Linguistic-Programming) technique called **The New Behavior Generator.**

After you read through the instructions a couple times, memorize the essence of the technique, and then close your eyes and run through the routine a couple of times. It's extremely powerful and works fast.

What you're about to do works in a very similar way to what athletes do when they mentally rehearse their sport in their mind before the big event. You can re-map your brain easily, using just your imagination.

The New Behavior Generator works by accessing a variety of representational systems, or the way in which you perceive the world. The main representational systems are visual (which is seeing) auditory (which is hearing), kinesthetic (which is touching or feeling), olfactory (your sense of smell), and gustatory (your sense of taste).

NLP is a set of methods anyone can use that will enable you to literally rewire the physical neurology within your brain so that you can become a more resourceful and effective human being.

The basis for this process is very simple. How you perceive reality dictates how you respond to it. Change your perception about an experience, and the behavior must change. It is a very powerful and easy way to make changes very quickly.

The New Behavior Generator:

Here's how the new behavior generator works:

Select a person who has the new behavior, i.e. the positive attitude that you would like to have. (The behavior you selected from step 4).

It can be anyone at all, someone you know or someone you admire from TV.

Think about a time when you saw this person acting in a way that best illustrates that new behavior you want.

Take a close look at how the person is behaving. Notice every detail about him or her, such as:

- Posture
- Breathing
- Facial expression
- Gestures
- Words that are used
- Tone of voice
- Eyes and eye movements

Imagine you are shadowing this person. You are moving behind them. Doing exactly what they do, moving the way they move, even thinking the way you imagine that they are thinking, and feeling the way you imagine they are feeling.

When you are perfectly satisfied that you are doing everything in just the same way, allow yourself to step inside of their body.

Now notice how it feels to be in their skin, as you continue to mimic their every word and gesture.

Notice how it feels to breathe as they are breathing and move as they are moving.

Notice how the world looks through their eyes and sounds in their ears.

Notice the way their muscles feel and feel their facial expression.

Feel what it's like to have their attitude about the world.

Notice how you feel about yourself as you act and behave in this way.

As you feel all of that, fully, imagine yourself in a future moment, behaving in this way.

Look around and notice where you are and what you see, as you behave in this new way. Notice the people around you and how they respond to you, behaving in this new way.

Repeat this routine several times.

Each time you run through the routine in your head, make it more and more real, but also do it quicker each time.

Congratulations! You did it! You have just moved from "victim thinking" to "empowered thinking"!

When you understand that you are the only one with the power, who's been responsible all along for creating the obstacles to good luck, then you realize that with that same power you can now go on to create whatever you want.

Chapter 4: Create Desire and Luck

There is nothing in the world that is more attractive to luck than your desire. There is something deep inside of you that you feel very passionate about. Whatever it is, this thing, for you, is in alignment with all your values.

You were born with many desires that are instinctive to being a human. Among them are your desire for survival, your desire for love, your desire for sexuality, your desire to belong, and your desire for recognition. There is, however, a desire that is one of the many infinite combinations of all desires that is special and unique to you as an individual.

You may find that you have many desires and wants in life. This is true for most people. The likeliness of creating luck grows the more you can focus on just one very meaningful desire at a time.

This desire is something that comes completely from within you and is not created by anything external to you. This special desire is born from your core values and becomes a driving force in your life.

You see, luck can look like so many things. It's a very individual process. A person who is worth billions of dollars and who is dying from cancer will find no value in coming into money. On the other hand, a young and healthy single mother, who has been out of work, would find no value in coming across some new information that could lead to a potential cure for cancer.

What is lucky for one person is completely meaningless to another. For you to find the potential for luck to exist in your life, you will first determine what is lucky to you, by understanding what it is you desire to receive in its favor.

You may think there are things that will bring happiness into your life. Things that may make you feel very comfortable. But are these your true desires in life? Will these things really make you happy? Are they coming from your true essence, your very heart and soul? Or are they ideas that have been passed on to you based on what other people think you should want, need, have, or desire?

Are religious beliefs, your parents' beliefs, or what your friends want or have filtering your desires? Are your desires being filtered by what you think is possible or what you think you should do? Are your desires needs or obsession-based? In other words, are you allowing unmet emotional needs for love, acceptance, or power to sway what you think you really desire?

Desire and obsession are two distinctly different feelings. Your desire can help you to manifest. It's an attractive positive feeling. On the other hand, obsession comes from a feeling of fear and lack, and is negatively charged. These negatively charged frequencies repel the very thing you think you want.

The want and need for someone's love and admiration, purely for the sake of ending your own loneliness, will not attract the right person to you. Yet, being an unconditionally loving person to all people and especially yourself and being an example of the type of person you wish to attract, increases your chances of being lucky in love.

Likewise, your want and need for money solely for the purpose of getting yourself out of debt, will not attract money to you. If you are a giving and resourceful person, who comes from a place of abundance and believes all people deserve to be abundant, rather than complaining or whining about how rich other people are and how bad you have it, you are being the type of person who can be lucky with money.

The funny thing is, the more you let go of your attachment and need for luck, the more luck you draw in.

Luck doesn't replace hard work, though. You will still work and take steps toward having your desires fulfilled. The difference is when you are doing work that feeds your soul, there is less struggle and far greater reward.

"The harder I work, the luckier I get."

~Samuel Goldwyn

Hard work doesn't seem like work at all when you are doing something that is coming from your deepest desire. That holds true for anything that you desire, whether it be a love relationship, creating world peace, a career, friendships, or traveling the world. All these things require effort, activity, and thought. But when you are in alignment with what your heart wants, you are flowing in natural harmony with the universe. The energy you put into things just comes natural to you, and you don't mind hard work in the least.

To drive the point home, you are luckiest when you know what your heart truly desires. You are even luckier the more you can pinpoint that thing and have a clear vision that you can easily articulate. You will draw in more lucky energy, just knowing what you want.

When you think about it, how can you be lucky when you haven't really defined what luck means to you?

Luck may, on the surface, appear to happen by mishap. But you absolutely can influence the force of luck to turn more in your favor, the more you choose to live in alignment with your desires. Instinctively you know how to be happy and no matter what your desire is, when you fulfill the true desires of your soul, you are at peace and you are abundant.

Exercise: Let all thoughts go for now and tap into your true inner wisdom, that part of you that knows what your soul wants.

Just take 5 – 15 minutes right now to close your eyes and ask yourself the following question:

"What do I really want?"

Imagine yourself in your ideal lucky situation in some area of your life, in whatever area you wish to become lucky.

Get in touch with what you really want, whether you think you can have it or not. Just allow yourself to dream about this for a little while.

Then, once an idea has popped into your head, I want you to **spend the next 5 – 15 minutes writing:**

The thing I desire the most right now is:

Just write and write and write as much as you can about it. I want you to completely empty your mind, writing from a positive, inspired place on what you DO desire. If you hear the words, "don't", "not", or "no", or any other negative words coming to your mind, I want you to immediately replace those words with their positive opposite replacement. You are creating what you DO desire, not getting rid of your "don't wants."

Take that time to get in touch with your true heart's desire now before moving on to the next lesson.

Chapter 5: Open to New Opportunity

I'm sure it's safe to assume that most people want to find opportunities, but only a few can recognize them and even fewer choose to act upon them.

Bill Gates is quoted as saying,

> *"There has never been a time like the present, with so many opportunities."*

What do you think? Do you think there are a lot of opportunities available? Take note of what your immediate reaction was to that question.

When it comes to opportunities, I want you to honestly look at yourself by asking these questions:

How much of your time is spent focusing on the negative side of life?

What's not working?

Are you being pessimistic, complaining, being cynical, or jealous over other people's success or opportunities?

Do you feel the world or people are working against you?

Do you feel you are or are not getting your fair share of what the world owes you?

Are you tired of the constant struggle?

What happens when you focus on the negative side of life instead of the positive is that you miss out on seeing the abundance of opportunities that is all around you.

What if you began seeing everything in your life as an opportunity?

What if you asked:

What is the significance of this situation?

What can I learn?

What if you saw all the problems you are presented with as a lucky opportunity for you to be the one to solve them?

The more resourceful you are, the more you insure your chance at luck.

Problems tell us that something in us wants to change. Many times, it's you that needs to change. If something about you is not working in a relationship, the sooner you can accept that and use that as a catalyst to change yourself, the sooner you can move on to enjoy the success of a relationship.

Problems just give us information. How we see them and what we do with them will make all the difference in whether a challenge turns into an opportunity, resulting in our good fortune or not. If you think about it, every model of a new business idea or product or service has stemmed from an issue or problem that someone tried to solve. If everyone just complained about the problem, rather than trying to come up with a solution, there wouldn't be any products or services to help people.

Every single product you see on the market today came about as a result of someone thinking something along the lines of: "There must be a better or more efficient way to do this."

Rather than focusing on the problems you face and feeling the frustration that arises when things don't work right, ask yourself:

Why was I presented with this problem?

Is there a solution?" (There always is!)

Could this be my opportunity to come up with a solution?

I'm not saying you'll be able to solve all problems easily, but when you approach it from a "What CAN I do" perspective, rather than "I can't do anything about this", you will eventually come up with ideas for each problem you face.

As you change your approach to problems, you widen your potential for opportunity to find you. If you change your approach like this, you will be open to opportunities worth exploring. If you continue thinking the same things and therefore doing the same things, you are going to keep getting the same things.

Opening to opportunities will require you to change your thinking. And therefore, luck IS within your control - because you can change the way you think, causing opportunities to begin suddenly to appear as if out of nowhere. They have been there all along, but you were blind to them.

Now you are opening parts of your brain that were literally shut down before, such that you were not able to see what was there. There are more opportunities available to you right now than you could ever imagine.

Try adding these assumptions to your enlightened filter system:

Everything that happens in my life is an opportunity for growth.

Every encounter is something from which I can learn.

As often as you possibly can, ask yourself:

What can I learn from this situation?

What can I do differently next time?

By adopting this more positive outlook, you naturally seek ways to learn and move forward. In turn, you discover that the world is not working against you; it is helping you to grow and move closer to your realized self.

Is this normal or comfortable? No! Growth is not normal and comfortable. What's normal is dysfunctional behavior. At least 70 – 80% of people grow up in dysfunctional families and watch their parents struggle to get by. Being comfortable is the opposite of stretching and growing.

You must be able to get beyond what is normal and comfortable. After all, isn't luck reserved for those fortunate people who belong to an exclusive members-only club called "The Lucky Few"? Do you think these people are normal? Luck is very abnormal.

What you will receive with your exclusive club membership to "The Lucky Few" is a new state of mind, which transcends the way normal people (that's the 80% of which are either broke, live in dysfunctional relationships, work at a dead end job, are divorced, are extremely obese, or suffering from some other stress-related ailment) think.

Lucky people do abnormal things. They are the ones who take the risks and go out on a limb and catch a lucky break. They are the ones who put themselves in a position to be able act quickly and seize those short, opportunity-filled moments.

Even if you see opportunities now, do you act on them? Or are you like most normal people who are scared or skeptical or waiting for the right time? At some point in your life, you're going to have to say "yes" to an opportunity.

You must put some of your faith into something working out in your favor. You must be willing to grab that luck. It's not as black and white as bending over and finding a million dollars lying on the ground. You must align yourself in such a way that you are attracting more and more opportunities.

Then at some point, or maybe even several points, you must decide to take a turn toward something that could turn out to be that big lucky break.

Measure the gravity of both answers: what's the worst that could happen if you say yes? And what's the worst that could happen if you say no? Remember, typically speaking, the rewards far outweigh the risks: the larger the risk, the larger the reward.

What if you put yourself out there and fail or things don't work out? You will have learned at least one thing. That way doesn't work. Now you know what didn't work. That information is valuable and gets you one step closer to something that will work.

"I am not discouraged,
because every wrong attempt
discarded is another step
forward."

~Thomas Edison

Questions to ask now:

- Are there any opportunities on the table right now that you have been thinking about taking advantage of but haven't?
- What is holding you back from moving forward?
- What's the worst that will happen if you do move forward?
- What's the worst that will happen if you don't?
- As you look back over your life, can you recall any moments when you thought in hindsight:

Oh, I wish I would have done that when I had the chance

If only I would have acted on that or acted sooner.

- What are some of those things?

List at least 5 times in your life when you let an opportunity pass you by:

1._____

2._____

3._____

4._____

5._____

"As you grow older, you'll find
the only things you regret are
the things you didn't do."

~Zachary Scott

"You miss 100% of the shots
you don't take."

~ Wayne Gretsky

Chapter 6: Learning From Your Past

Some experiences from our past create what are called generalizations, which are basically limiting beliefs. Limiting beliefs cause us to repeat the same patterns of behavior repeatedly. If you continue repeating the same behavior patterns, you are certain of one thing, repeating the same results.

In the last chapter, we talked about being open to opportunities.

I asked you to: "list at least 5 points in your life when you let an opportunity pass you by". I hope you did make that list, because we're going to be using that information in this chapter. If you have already done that, awesome! Well done! You are getting the point of my message.

If you haven't, it's understandable. You just haven't quite grasped the importance or sense of urgency necessary to change your luck for the better. You see, most normal people will just read my book, or listen to this program, and unfortunately, they won't do anything different.

Hence, they will not attract good luck. These are the people who are still waiting and hoping to land upon the genie in my book that pops out and sprinkles all the magic fairy dust on them, granting them many wishes and pointing them toward a rainbow which leads to a pot of gold at the end.

It reminds me of how many people I meet who are so impressed by the success of my hypnosis website, www.hyptalk.com. They see a petite, modest, yet good-looking gal, with a successful Internet business and ask, "Hey do you think you can show me how to create a wildly successful website like yours, Victoria? I want to do exactly what you do. I have a great idea to do such-and-such on the Internet. What's the secret of your success?"

On the inside, I take a deep breath, sigh, chuckle a little, and think, *"Forgive them, for they know not what they're suggesting, or asking."*

I doubt very seriously that most people would really want to do exactly what I do, if they knew how I spend most of my days. I'm not complaining because I do love what I do. I am extremely passionate about what I do. I'm just saying that there is much more hard work and figuring things out going on behind the scenes than meets the eye.

At first, I used to entertain this question by going into a few of the details of what needs to be done - the market research, keyword research, learning how to set up a blog or a website, a youtube.com channel, a Twitter profile, getting certified, getting a business license, a webhost, etc., etc. Before I could even begin to scratch the surface about the thousands upon thousands of hours of hard work and dedication that has gone into building this business, I begin to see their eyes glaze over as if I'm telling them a bedtime story.

I've seriously thought about writing a book about Internet Marketing because I realize I do have a lot to offer in that area. But the truth is, there are already so many other books offered on that topic. I'd just be repeating the same information that's readily available and has been suggested by people who are much more talented than me, and far more capable of explaining the technical aspects of it.

When it comes down to it, only those who seriously dedicate themselves to the material found in those books will be able to create a successful Internet business. The truth is, Internet success, mine or anyone else's for that matter, doesn't always follow a cut and dry formula. It goes way deeper than any instruction manual I could put together. It's about mindset. I knew nothing about developing websites or marketing at all when I started my Internet Company. What made me successful was that I knew the result I wanted to create. I saw no alternative for myself other than making that happen. I figured out everything completely as a result of my drive to succeed. I turned what many would have considered a bad day into my lucky opportunity.

Let me take you back to when I started Hyptalk.com in 1999. Little did I know at the time that it was my final few months as a stockbroker. I decided I was going to start my own business on the side, so I became certified in hypnosis and hypnotherapy. It all happened so fast and furiously that within four months of being certified as a hypnotherapist, I was getting my business license, which required leasing office space, which somehow lead to setting up advertising in the yellow pages and local newspapers. This was all before making a single dollar in my practice.

My branch manager at the time caught wind of my audacious plans and presented me with an ultimatum to either quit the brokerage business, from which I made a steady six-figure-a-year income or give up on my no-income business venture. I had no prior business skills. As a matter of fact, my stock brokerage experience was my first real job in sales. I had investments I'd have to leave on the table. I was to decide within 30 days.

I think we all know what decision I chose. Looking back on that situation, I would not change one thing about it. That was my lucky opportunity! It was the push I needed. I never have to ask myself "what if?" because I know my life took a turn toward a direction that is more in alignment with who I really am.

Now, in 2012 as my 13th anniversary of self-employment approaches, I look over the decisions I have made as a business owner. I ask myself the same question I ask you: Are there points in my life where I have allowed opportunities to pass me by?

Yes, of course there have been. Many business people approach me and want me to look at an opportunity. I'll admit that I am very protective of the company I have built, and as such, I have turned down most of the proposals I have been offered. I can have extreme tunnel vision about my business at times. Have I allowed opportunities to pass me by? Could they have worked out in my favor and made my path a little easier? Maybe. Now, it does take a little humility to admit this, just as it may take a little on your part. We all have something we can learn from our past about what has worked and what we might have done differently.

I've been vulnerable with you and I have shared my story. Now it's your turn to be vulnerable with yourself and share your story.

You know, none of this stuff is extremely comfortable at first. I wish everyone who buys and reads my book would take out their pens and notepads and write down some notes and put in the necessary work. But history tells us that not everyone will put the time and energy into it.

But YOU will, won't you?

All right, enough about that already. I'll stop belaboring the point and get on with it.

For this chapter, which is critical to you changing your luck, to do anything for you at all, you do need to have at least one of those opportunities you let pass you by at your disposal for the purpose of this exercise.

If you're thinking you never get opportunities or let them pass you by, think again. Every exercise in this book is an opportunity.

Invest some time in yourself right now. You're not doing this for me. You're doing it because you want to change your relationship with luck in your life. This chapter will cause you to literally change your past and help you to truly be open to new opportunities and seize upon those lucky chances in your future.

We're going to use another NLP technique called "Change Personal History," which was originally developed by Dr. John Grinder and Dr. Richard Bandler. This technique will allow you the opportunity to redo past events, experiencing yourself as if you had known then what you know now. The process re-maps your brain so that you are programmed to behave in the way you would now be behaving given the new context of your old experience. It's magical how it works.

Don't worry; we're not literally going to change your past or create false memories. What we are doing is somewhat like what would happen if you were watching TV and you wanted to adjust the brightness or the color or the sound. You're still going to be watching the same exact show but watching it in a new way that enhances your experience of the program and how you respond to it.

You need to have about 15 minutes available where you will not be disturbed to do this technique.

Let's begin:

Recall a time from your past when you passed up a potentially lucky opportunity. Even if you don't know for sure how it would have turned out, that's just fine ... Just bring that situation or event to your mind ... and more important than the situation itself, experience the feeling ... maybe it's Uncertainty? Fear? Feeling overwhelmed? Lack of confidence? Lack of trust? Apathy? Maybe it's a combination of those feelings or some other feelings that cause you to pass up potentially lucky opportunities. Just experience that feeling ... and on a scale from 1-10 [10 being the most] how intense is that feeling?

Now you'll create what's called an anchor to this state by squeezing your thumb and forefinger on your right hand together while you are feeling the feelings at their peak. Then you'll release your right-hand thumb and forefinger and shake it off to break the state. Blink your eyes a few times. Take a couple deep breaths. Just completely shake off the state.

To re-enter that state again now, go ahead and press your right thumb and forefinger together again, and as you do, imagine yourself stepping onto an imaginary timeline that has your past to your left and your future to your right, with you standing in the present moment.

Now go back to an even earlier time when you experienced that same feeling by floating over your timeline and noticing any other memories of times when you've passed up opportunities that may have become lucky for you. Just notice where you go and notice your experience, and then go back to an even earlier memory.

Continue moving back through your past timeline, recalling similar times in your life, and experiencing the feeling, until you have finally reached your earliest experience of that feeling or state that causes you to pass up on potentially lucky opportunities.

Release your right-hand thumb and forefinger …

Now … go ahead and completely break your state by shaking it off again, blink a few times, breathe deeply, let it go, and come back to the present moment.

Now I want you, knowing what you know now, to think about the way you would like to have been able to respond in those moments that would have made a positive impact. A way to respond that would have allowed you to be open and receptive to the new idea and to take a necessary risk, for you to reap the reward. Think about an appropriate resource that would have made a significant difference to the quality of the earliest experience. Perhaps you might want to have the confidence, the trust, the passion, or even the knowledge you now have that you did not have then.

Now, once you're in touch with that resource or that state, go ahead and anchor that resource by squeezing your left thumb and forefinger as you fully associate with the resourceful feeling state, pressing your thumb and forefinger together only when that state has reached its peak. Hold it and release it.

Perhaps if you float up back over your past timeline, there were times that you did take a chance that turned out in your favor … float over your time line, and if you do find any actual times where you did access this state, notice those times as well, and anchor those feelings in your thumb and forefinger.

What other resource would you like to have had? Continue anchoring as many of these resources to your left-hand thumb and forefinger, squeezing them together each time you access a peak state of a beneficial resource. And release your thumb and forefinger and relax. Open your eyes and blink a couple of times; take a deep breath and let it go.

Now let's revisit that earliest experience, where you passed up an opportunity. Connect with that old memory again, and now fire the resource anchor by pressing your left thumb and forefinger together. And allow this new state you've just created to reside right there in the place of the old non-resourceful state. You should feel a shift in your energy back then, making you feel all the resources that would have been needed back then for you to feel like you could make a different choice.

If you are not satisfied with the change, break the state and come back to the present and find more new resources to add to your anchor. Then return to the past and fire off the anchor again.

When you are fully satisfied and feel yourself reliving that old memory with the new feelings, then simply move forward toward the present, carrying with you the new resources and firing off that anchor into each of those memories we originally went through.

Once you have reached the present moment, break your state. Now remember the past experiences and notice if, when you remember them, you now feel more resourceful.

Future pace: Now, recall a future situation where you may have normally found yourself in the old way, but as you step into the future, become aware of whether you are applying your new resources in those future moments.

Well done!

Chapter 7: Acknowledging the Luck in Your Life

The next part of the process of attracting good luck is acknowledging the luck you already have in your life. Now, you may have to reach back into the far recesses of your brain to come up with some things, but you could also probably come up with some things that have happened even just this week if you really think about it. You can acknowledge the big things you have in your life and even the small things.

Everything you have in your life is a direct result of luck by the mere definition of opportunity meeting with action. We're now talking about those opportunities that you HAVE acted upon. I tell you this: as soon as you start appreciating the lucky experiences you have already had and acknowledge the luck you do have in your life, you will realize just how lucky you are.

Of course, you want even more luck. Do not mistake my point to be that I'm helping you to turn your luck around merely by showing you where you are already lucky. What I am talking about here is one of the main principles found in the Law of Attraction.

In case you are not already familiar with the Law of Attraction, it states that like energy attracts like energy. There's a bit more to it than that, but if you will, consider that your emotions are energy and each type of emotion you have, whether it be positive or negative, is charged with an energy vibration. Positive emotions are charged positively, and negative emotions are charged negatively.

Broken down even further, there are varying degrees of positive emotion, each producing higher and higher energy vibrations. Positive emotions range on a scale from contentment being only slightly charged, to hopeful, optimistic, and all the way up to the highest positive emotions, which all carry the strongest vibration. Those are love, empowerment, freedom, joy, and appreciation. Appreciation is another word for gratitude. Simply put, having the feeling of gratitude helps you to raise your energy vibration.

By feeling grateful for the luck, you already do have, you are going to put yourself into the proper mindset to attract more of it. When you are in a state of truly feeling gratitude for what you have, there is no higher energy vibration that attracts other similar opportunities your way.

Looking at this even from a purely functional, non-ethereal, common sense standpoint, it stands to reason that whatever you focus on is going to expand. Even the most logical-minded person, could get behind that, right?

If you are thinking to yourself, "I am so unlucky," your awareness shifts to accommodate that belief by filtering your perception to only allow you to be able to recognize the lack of luck in your life. It's true. You have so much data coming at you; it's impossible to pay attention to everything your senses take in. Your subconscious mind does a brilliant job of sorting out the information and bringing you things that match what is already recognizable to you, so that you can make sense of it all. Your beliefs play a huge role in this sorting-out process. If you're familiar with a way of thinking, your mind will tend to skew whatever you hear and see and match it up with things that validate your way of thinking.

Most people are not thinking, "I'm so lucky." The mind is not looking for ways to validate the lucky-thought process. It's looking for ways to validate not being lucky. That's what is familiar and comfortable and real in their mind. But if you shift your focus to thinking of yourself as lucky, you are naturally going to have a lucky-level awareness that looks for more opportunities to strengthen the idea that you are lucky.

You see, we're all dealing with the same data. Two sales people can work for the very same company. One makes $10,000 in sales a month consistently month after month. The other makes $100,000 consistently month after month. You might say that the $100,000 per month employee gets all the luck. And you'd be right, based on our definition: Opportunity meeting Action. The $100,000 sales person recognizes lucky opportunities more often. There's some intuition going on there as well, which we'll get into in another chapter. But the sales person who does the $100,000 expects it to happen and therefore creates it. The

$100,000 a month sales person, says: "Look at all my past great sales. I did such a great job last month; I'm going to do an even better job next month."

The $10,000 per month sales person says, "Look at that $100,000 sales person. They get all the luck. Look at me. Nothing good ever comes my way." That one complains about not only their misfortune, but the fortune of others as well.

This way of thinking creates nothing but a downward spiral. Not only are you feeling sorry for yourself, but you are also programming your subconscious mind to think poorly about people who do well. You're programming your subconscious mind to believe that there are only so many opportunities, and that person is somehow stealing them all from you.

You must stop this way of thinking immediately and begin to look at what you do have as opposed to what you don't have. Not only that, you also would be wise to send a different message to your subconscious mind when something good happens to somebody else. I challenge you to not only be grateful for those things, while they may seem smaller in direct proportion to what everyone else has, if you give them enough attention, focus, and gratitude, those things are going to grow; but when someone else gets that success you want, be grateful and happy for their success too.

I know that may seem like a lot to swallow, but when you can genuinely feel happy that someone else has succeeded, you are telling yourself that there are a lot of opportunities to go around. When you see someone else succeed, be happy for them because they opened a door for you to better yourself.

Whatever you are thinking about that person, you are ultimately saying to yourself, "They really deserved that success," and at the same time, you are telling yourself, "I also deserve to succeed." The trick is to really mean it. Your feelings don't lie. See yourself as no less and no more deserving than others who are succeeding. Perhaps there is something you can learn from them. By congratulating them and being happy for them and authentically looking to the experience, maybe there is something you could learn and grow from.

"They" say, "Don't count your blessings." I'm saying, it's time to start counting them and watching them multiply as a result.

When you DO focus on what you have created, you are entering a state of mind that is resourceful. You are feeling good about yourself, having faith, and believing things can happen. You have your eyes open now to new possibilities.

Whether you believe in the Law of Attraction on a cellular level of energy being attracted to like energy or not, you simply cannot argue with the fact that when you feel good, and think helpful thoughts, you are more attractive to others and you are more resourceful.

Having gratitude for the opportunities that have resulted in luck is one of the best ways to bring about more of those opportunities.

That brings us to this next exercise:

I want you **to write down at least 10 lucky opportunities you are grateful for.** For example, if you have children, do you feel lucky to have such wonderful kids in your life who bring you so much joy? Think about everything that had to go perfectly right in your life, just to create such a beautiful miracle. What about the other relationships in your life? What about your job(s) or career(s) you have had or now have?

Those are the biggies.

What about the small, fortunate things that have happened to you? Have you received a gift or anything lately? Has someone take you out to lunch? Were you able to find something at the store on sale that you were looking for? Have you received a gift card, a gift certificate for even $10? Anything you can think of qualifies. Maybe you opened a piece of mail that was lucky, got an email or a lucky phone call. Did you win something? Did you get the perfect seats at a movie or a concert? It's not necessarily the quality of the experience that is important. Right now, we are looking at the sheer abundance of opportunities that you have been able to take advantage of

Go ahead. I'm sure you can come up with at least 10 things to list.

~Welcome back~

How are you feeling now?

If you did the exercise as I was hoping, you are probably feeling just a little bit more hopeful and realize that you have had some success with luck already. Again, remember the point of the exercise is not to settle and just be happy with what you have. The point is to raise your vibration to a higher level and gain that sense of empowerment about your ability to attract good luck as you notice the luck that is already in and all around you.

Chapter 8: Be Prepared – Are you Ready for Luck?

As you are starting to see, there is already a significant amount of luck that has gone unnoticed in your life. Perhaps there have been plenty of opportunities that you know you could have taken advantage of, but for one reason or another, you just weren't in the right frame of mind to take advantage of it, or you didn't trust yourself enough to act.

Many opportunities are available, and the more you can recognize the many chances that come your way, and the more open you are to those chances, the more potential you will have to increase your luck.

Luck comes as a result of acting upon an opportunity. You must be able to see the opportunities, but you also need to be able to take advantage of them. If a lucky opportunity comes your way and you don't have the resources to take advantage of it, you have no way to turn it into luck, do you?

There are several things that go into being prepared, which can mean completely different things to different people at different times. In a lot of ways, it can mean just having a mindset for preparedness. For example, you can determine in your mind that you will be ready to act quickly, should the right opportunity come your way. You cannot predict the future or every scenario that is going to come along, but have you considered some of the more likely scenarios that could happen? Furthermore, have you thought about what you would do in the given scenario?

If the right opportunity came your way, are you prepared to take advantage of it? Let's say, for example, you are looking to start a new shopping business online. Perhaps you require a sophisticated website and a marketing strategy to get things off the ground. By sheer luck, you meet someone who happens to be a genius at building business websites or a very successful marketing guru who's willing to split the investment with you, giving you the opportunity to cut your costs by half! Now, all that is standing between you and your success is an investment of, say, $10,000, or whatever the amount may be. Do you have the capital, which, in this case, is the action needed to turn this rare opportunity into luck? You may not necessarily have the money sitting in your bank account right now, but do you can put together the capital through friends, family, loans, etc.?

Let's take the idea of getting into a relationship. Relationships require another kind of investment. They require an investment of time, but they also require an emotional investment. If the man or woman of your dreams suddenly became available, are you truly ready in every way to meet this person? Or are you still dealing with getting over a prior relationship? Do you have physical hang-ups about your body that might make you feel less confident about dating this person? Are your personal and business affairs organized enough that you have the time to invest in getting to know someone without sacrificing your work or your children or other areas of your life?

What if your dream home suddenly became available at an amazingly "bargain" price? Are you in a position to make that purchase? What if an all-expense paid vacation to your favorite place on earth was presented to you? Do you have the time to take advantage of it?

You see, you need to be available and ready to act upon the opportunities that come your way, for them to be of any value. Have you given much thought to your desired outcomes and considered what you would do if presented with a scenario?

Sadly, too many opportunities are allowed to pass by because people are just not prepared for them when they arise.

Consider the following questions:

Are you...

- Always running late?
- Emotionally unavailable; i.e., not over an ex?
- In debt over your head?
- Suffering with addictions?
- Always sick or tired or achy?
- Dealing with legal matters?

These and other similar situations are roadblocks to your chances for attracting good luck.

Remember, the Law of Attraction works on the premise that like attracts like. Whatever luck you are trying to create, you need to become a conduit for that luck.

For example, if you are trying to become lucky in love, think about what it is you want to attract. Do you want someone who physically attractive? Then you need to be someone who works to be physically attractive, since healthy people who take care of themselves are probably looking for someone who does the same. That's what I mean by "being prepared".

If you are trying to start a business, think about all the possible ways you could attract an investor or customers to your business. Are you ready for customers to start asking you questions? Are you prepared with answers to those questions? Are you ready to put money into the right opportunity? Do you have the time? It's time to begin really examining your readiness.

You do not have to have ALL your ducks in a row and everything completely sorted out in your life in order to take advantage of a lucky opportunity that comes along, but you do need to be realistic about what is happening or not happening in your life right now. You need to have some sort of foundation to build upon. Whatever is broken in your life right now is taking time, energy, thought, and probably some money to keep it that way.

If your physical health is in turmoil, how are you going to be able to act in the love department? Or how will you undertake a business endeavor that will require a lot of your energy?

If you're broke and up to your ears in debt, it would be a very irresponsible proposition to put yourself further into debt in order to take advantage of even the best opportunities available to you.

If you're working three jobs and have no time to spend even with yourself, how will you find the time to dedicate to a relationship?

Now is the time to prepare yourself by taking care of whatever is broken in your life. Here's where I want you to make a list of some things that need to be taken care of. You need to create the best version of you possible for you to live your best life possible.

As a society, we often think about worst-case scenarios and do what we can to prepare for them. Here in Florida, where I live, our whole community goes through the same ritual every year, around the beginning of June. We make sure we have enough bottled water, canned goods, flashlights, radios, shutters, etc. to get us through in the event of a hurricane. In Washington, where I grew up, though, we had a few earthquakes and fires. As children we ran through the "what if" scenario as the drill bell would ring. We'd get down under our desks, as if we were having an earthquake, or calmly walk single file to the assigned location in case of a fire.

I'm sure every area has its own set of preparedness rituals. These are all to prepare for an unlikely worst-case scenario. Well, what's being done to prepare for the best-case scenario? Probably not a whole lot of thought has gone into this. What if we started thinking, "How do I become the perfect match for opportunity?"

I want you to create a personal assessment of your life. This personal assessment is an ongoing assignment. You may be able to list a few things right now, but this is the type of thing you are going to find more and more answers to over the next month or so, as you become more aware of your life.

This assessment is to include these four areas:

- Health
- Money
- Relationships
- Environment

The questions to ask yourself is, "What am I putting up with in these areas?"

You are going to create a list of every frustrating thing that you are dealing with. For example, next month, when a bill comes in and you feel stressed about it because it's too high, or you don't have the money for it, or maybe it's a subscription you forgot to cancel — whatever the reason — write it down.

Maybe it's that broken appliance in your kitchen. Write it down.

Maybe it's that you can't fit into anything, or you feel like you don't have anything to wear.

Maybe it's that back pain or neck pain.

Maybe it's that it's Friday night, and you are lonely, and you have no one to hang out with. Or it could also be that you work so hard that you don't make time to get together with anyone.

Whatever you are putting up with, if it causes you any negative thought at all, write it down. I want you to keep writing things down on this list of things that you are putting up with in your life because this is going to become your "to-do" list — your checklist of things to do to get prepared.

Don't worry about how long this list is. It is not going to prevent or get in the way of you having what you want, and again, you do not have to fix everything in order to attract luck.

This list is just a bit of a reality check to help you to start strengthening your personal foundation. Has it been years since you've been to your dentist or doctor? Write these things down! Is that computer you're on slow and buggy? Write it down!

But don't just write these things down, check them off!

Anything else you know of that is standing in the way of your dreams and desires, write those things down too. This list is going to work as a best-case scenario preparedness kit. The more things you get checked off your list, the more prepared you are.

But something else is going to happen as well. Your self-confidence is going to go through the roof! Confidence comes as a result of knowing that you can accomplish anything. And as you see the items on your list getting checked off one by one, making your life better, easier, and more efficient, you feel better about yourself. You feel you deserve the good things in life. Your life flows easier, and you have more energy. You can put things into perspective because you don't have to expend energy on all those distractions, and each distraction or frustration you eliminate from your life makes more room for better things to happen in its place.

Bob Proctor said something I will always remember:

"Nature abhors a vacuum. If you don't have enough of what you want in your life, you have to make room for it by letting go of the things you no longer need"

You've experienced this every time you've cleaned out a closet or a cabinet, and though it may be sparse for a little while, soon it fills back up again with new stuff.

By letting go of the stuff that is holding you back from your future, you can begin to fill up those areas with things that are going to propel you toward the life you really want as you intentionally make yourself ready to take advantage of the desired lucky scenario.

Keep in mind, there is rarely ever a second chance to make a first impression. Whether that first impression is to a potential business partner, employer, friend, life partner, investor, talent scout, or customer, you typically get one shot at putting your best foot forward. In nearly all cases of lucky opportunities, another human being is somehow involved in the process, and thereby, you will be faced with someone else's personal assessment of you as a person. You may never know for sure when you are going to make that impression. It may be at a party or at a grocery store. If you arrive at those places, caught off guard with no business cards, or wearing your sweatpants, you may have blown your opportunity.

The point is that somewhere along the way, you are going to find yourself in a situation that could turn out to be the one lucky opportunity you've been looking for.

Will you be ready?

Chapter 9: Waking up to Opportunities

There will be an abundance of chance encounters that will come your way, and you will now know exactly how to make use of them because you are going to create the ability to become more mentally alert with razor-sharp thinking. The more mentally alert you are, the easier it is for you to make quick and intelligent decisions, and you will have the wherewithal to act upon information and ideas immediately.

Your thoughts and actions resulting from your increased mental alertness and awareness help you to recognize many more favorable opportunities than ever before. Part of this mental alertness simply comes from your own intuition, which you are becoming more and more in tune with. You listen to your own internal voice, or perhaps for you it's a feeling in your gut that gives you a strong feeling that this is right for you or this is wrong for you. Another way that you notice your intuition is that you may get a strong image in your mind of the result that would follow by acting on an idea.

As you gain more self-understanding and self-respect, your intuition is increased. And how does one go about self-understanding? By becoming aware — by really paying attention to all your senses. The more awake, alert, and energetic you are, the more you will be able to pay attention to all these things.

Your ability to take positive action toward a chance that is favorable for you is being strengthened through heightening your mental alertness, which is that tension, that impulse, that makes you act on a given situation.

One of the best ways I know of to create mental alertness is by taking extremely good care of yourself. You do this simply because you have self-respect — you respect your mind and your body. Since your mind and body are connected, when you strengthen your body, you are also strengthening your mind. Your mind is capable of so much more than you can ever imagine, and your sharp, heightened ability to think quickly and clearly is crucial to your ability to act upon the luck that you are attracting to yourself.

There is a rhythm of nature that you will begin to see as you truly pay attention. It is in everything — the rhythm of your heartbeat, your breathing, your eyes blinking, and the way the world turns. It's in the music that you hear; it's in the stars and every living organism. The same holds true with luck. Luck flows with this natural rhythm, and as you are becoming more in touch with the rhythm of nature and becoming more alert and aware of all the things going on around you, you recognize and are prepared for the cycle of luck as it flows in and all around you.

This means that you must align yourself and become more in step with nature. Pay attention to your body's need for plenty of rest; find out just how much sleep is right for you and respect your body's need for sleeping the right amount for you. Sleep when your body says sleep.

Chapter 10: Intuition – Taking Chances but Reducing Risk

Of course, it stands to reason that intuition plays a huge role in the luck you have in your life. If you can tune into that inner voice that tells you that something is good, or something is bad, you will greatly improve your luck.

One of the best ways I know of to enhance your intuition is by going into meditation or hypnosis daily and paying attention to your thoughts, your feelings, and all your senses. Are you aware of your inner voice? Do you pay attention to it? This voice softly whispers ideas and suggestions to you. Of course, that requires stepping out of your comfort zone, and for some people, that is to be avoided at all costs! (Even if the cost is living a life of mediocrity instead of the life of your dreams.)

Everyone has two different versions of their inner voice. The first is called intuition. This is a quiet whisper that tries to tell us things that are good for us. The second one could be called our gremlin. This one is a bit louder and tells us what is bad or wrong about ourselves. Sadly, the latter voice is the one most of us are aware of and pay attention to. The gentler one, that is our intuition, is often ignored — if we're hearing what it tells us at all. The great pity here is that our intuition really has our best interests at heart. Our gremlin (the louder, more aggressive voice) does have our welfare at heart too, but in a protective way. The intuition is way is more expansive.

What is wrong with protecting ourselves? I do hear you thinking that! Well, it limits us and ultimately erodes our well-being at a soul level. And believe it or not, but that is not good for our physical or emotional well-being! If you're unfulfilled at a soul level, you will slowly and imperceptibly develop a nagging feeling of general discontent that can have a rippling effect on your mood, self-esteem, and - ultimately - your physical and mental health. But that is for another article.

The gentle voice of your intuition will, if listened to, stretch you beyond your comfort zone, but never more than you're capable of. It will challenge you, but also support you. It always has your best interests at heart at every level: physically, mentally, emotionally, and spiritually. It will not only gently nudge you in scary directions, which will yield huge and unimaginable rewards, but it will also gently warn when to stop or turn around.

When you tune into your intuition and allow yourself to be guided by it, you will be surprised at how much easier formerly assumed "challenges" will become, how much good fortune lands in your lap (we call it synchronicity), and how good you feel being at ease with yourself and all your life experiences, even the ones you wouldn't choose!

If you're not used to listening to your intuition, learning to tune into it will require time and patience. At first, you may be unsure which voice is which (especially as your gremlin often sounds very reasonable), and using your intuition is very much like using your physical muscles. You need to use it regularly for it to be in good working shape.

So how do you get to know your intuition better? First, start to watch out for hunches, feelings, or ideas that crop up. Pay attention to the voice that accompanies them. Is it gentle, positive, and supportive? If it is aggressive, domineering, or uses scare-mongering tactics, it is more likely to be your gremlin. If you're getting a feeling of warning, ask yourself if it is a loud and threatening one (gremlin) or an insistent, "knowing" one (intuition).

The scary thing about trusting your intuition when it is new to you is that it is not based on logic, and often, what it suggests to you cannot be justified logically. But with practice and trust, you'll learn that "knowing" that something is the right thing to do is in your best interest. It'll be easier to shrug off your own gremlin and that of others who will fear for your best interests on your behalf.

The key to developing the all-essential trust is to start small. Don't make life-changing decisions based on your intuition if you're not familiar with it (you might still be confusing your two inner voices). Do ask your intuition to guide you with smaller decisions and wait for the gentle, knowing feeling to arrive. Don't expect an instant answer but watch out for it. It will come, and you'll know it when it does.

Over time, as you tune in more and more, you'll find you suffer less and less with worry or anxiety. You'll trust that all will work out well, and often you'll find it works out better than you could ever have imagined!

The more you can tune into and trust your intuition, the more success you are going to have in all areas of your life, especially concerning your luck.

Chapter 11: Belief

"Whether you believe you can,
or you believe you can't, either
way you're probably right."

— Henry Ford

Understanding your beliefs, how they control your life, and the limitations caused by beliefs are key ingredients in attracting good luck.

What are beliefs?

Very simply, beliefs are those things that we believe to be true. Beliefs are personal. What we believe is not the same as what other people believe. Two people can look at the same thing and have different beliefs about it, and they both can be right at the same time. Yet our limited perspective has us believing that only our own beliefs are right while everyone who believes differently is wrong!

Beliefs are formed throughout your life. They are mostly created from our experiences or what we have heard other people suggest before. You establish your beliefs by copying people you respect, as a result of repetitive events, or even single, very emotional or traumatic events. In many cases, our beliefs are hypnotic suggestions, which we received from a very early age from our parents. We heard our parents suggest at a time before the logic and reasoning part of our brain is fully developed, and so we believe everything irrefutably up until the age of around six years old.

You can also pick up beliefs from your culture and your environment. You will have some beliefs for your entire life while beliefs about other things may be changed several times during your life.

We read books, and we believe what we read in those books. You can hear one person share something with you about something they believe, and it can very quickly become the set way that you believe about that thing from then on.

What's important to understand here is that MOST of the things we believe are not factual. A fact provides scientific evidence such as the fact that gravity will cause objects to fall to the ground. This is indisputable and believed by all of humanity. However, most beliefs are not so clearly defined; they pertain to us and our perspective of the world. Things we believe are subjective, such as who we are, how we should act in certain situations, what is good for us, what is bad for us, who we can trust, and who likes us.

What do beliefs do for us?

Beliefs are like a lens through which we look at the world. They fundamentally distort, reshape, and change the importance of the information that we take in through our senses, thereby creating the view that we really have of the world.

Beliefs have a strong effect on your behavior: if you believe you should do something or think something then you usually end up doing or thinking it!

Beliefs strongly influence both what you do and what you learn from your environment; it is difficult for you to learn anything or do anything that you believe is going to be unpleasant or bad for you.

"If you believe you can, or you believe you can't, either way, you're right."

~Henry Ford

Beliefs not only shape your view of the world, but they also control the way that you react.

An example of this is the well-known medical placebo effect in which something as simple as water can, in fact, be as effective as the real drug, if you believe that you're taking the real drug.

We've seen that beliefs can shape our world by affecting the way we perceive it and by affecting the way that we react to it. We have also seen how powerful they can be. This can make them a fantastic tool for you or a mortal enemy.

Positive beliefs that support your goals and values will produce very positive results for you. However, through no fault of your own, you have almost certainly acquired some limiting beliefs during your childhood.

Limiting beliefs often begin with you saying to yourself, "I can't." They may even have been true at some point in your life or are still true today. The danger is that you are likely to automatically apply these beliefs to the rest of your life, jeopardizing your future and your success.

For example, it may be true that you don't know how to do something today, but so often, the way that you express this is by saying, "I can't do it". If you say that often enough, it becomes a belief, and as you've seen, this belief becomes the truth.

Even worse are limiting beliefs, which are not based on the truth but on some belief that has been instilled into you by your parents, your friends, or society. If you believe that you're destined to be poor or that you're not capable of attracting money or good luck, well then, that is the inevitable outcome.

Give your beliefs a check-up

For the next seven days, I would like you to think very carefully about your beliefs; watch yourself as you interact with people. Look for those "I can't" statements. Identify them, write them down, and ask yourself just how much harm they are doing. Do you really want to let them kill your chance of attracting good luck?

Every time you find yourself making one of those "I can't" statements, turn it into a "How can I...?" question. "I can't attract more money" becomes "How can I attract more money?" Can you feel the difference? If you do this consistently, you'd better believe that you will see the difference in your life! Where there's a will, there's a way!

1) Affirmations

An affirmation is the firm declaration of something to be true and is intended to convince the mind that what it wants to happen will happen. For example, stating repeatedly, "I can get any job I want," is intended to instill in the mind the confidence to go out and get any job that it wants. This resembles the Law of Attraction, but it is not enough to sway the subconscious until other methods are employed as well.

Wikipedia describes affirmation this way (I found this interesting since it shows very well how affirmation and the Law of Attraction are joined together and would not have been the same if it was altered in any way):

"In spirituality and personal development, an affirmation is a form of autosuggestion in which a statement of a desirable intention or condition of the world or the mind is deliberately meditated on and/or

repeated in order to implant it in the mind. Many believers recommend accompanying recitations with mental visualization of a desired outcome. Affirmation could be viewed positively as a mobilization of one's inner resources, or negatively as a kind of self-induced brainwashing, depending on the psychological depth and wisdom of the affirmation. For example, believers would consider, 'I am making more room in my life for success every day,' a much wiser affirmation than, 'I will win the lottery today!' Affirmations are always phrased in the first person and usually in a present tense (I am) rather than a future tense (I will) in order to increase the realization of the statement for the affirmer."

Affirmations are believed to be a very powerful means of reprogramming the unconscious mind. They appear to be most effective when repeated in a quiet and restful state of mind and body, and when the desired outcome is vividly experienced in one's mind and resulting emotions are felt. They are an intrinsic part of many New Age groups including I AM Activity and the Church Universal and Triumphant of Elizabeth Clare Prophet. However, in these groups, affirmations are generally recited in flat, monotone voices at top speed and volume in order to elevate participants' "vibratory levels".

Perhaps the most often used and well-known affirmation is the word "Amen," which can be translated simply as "so be it" or "and so it is," affirming the truth of whatever was written or said immediately prior.

While often used to conclude prayer, the word itself is neutral as to its context and exemplifies a logical affirmation more than a spiritual one.

2) Visualization

Visualization works in much the same way as affirmation; you visualize yourself achieving something and your brain will come to believe it is so; therefore, you will be able to do it. Again, this is closely related to the Law of Attraction but does not address any underlying issues that could contribute to negative vibes.

Chapter 12: Set Your Intention to Create Luck

Your thoughts must be backed by positive emotion: the more powerful the emotion, the stronger the thought. It is essential to create within yourself the same feelings that you will have when you achieve your desire. You already do this all the time, only in the opposite direction. For example, you think of what you are afraid may happen and suddenly you feel frightened, tense and may even start to exhibit some physiological symptoms such as sweating, shaking, or shivering.

Begin to reverse this method of thinking. Think only of the positivity you want to create and conjure up the feelings associated with those thoughts. How will it feel to meet and marry that person of your dreams? How will it feel to sit behind the wheel of that brand-new Mercedes or to be standing in the kitchen of your dream home?

Powerful goals are exciting and electrifying. Clear intentions energize and propel you to move forward. Without clear intentions, you don't get around to doing the things that are really important to you because you end up spending your time putting out fires. You are left only to react to things that end up happening by default. Anything can happen if you don't intend specifically for the things that you want to happen. As the saying goes, if you fail to plan, you plan to fail.

Intention puts you in charge. You are steering your life in the direction you want it to go. Your intention is sort of like your mission statement. An intention statement can be a large or small goal that you desire to accomplish within a specific amount of time. It's a bit more than just saying, "I'm going to do this and this," and then just waiting to see if it happens.

Make no mistake; what happens is your intention. There are really no accidents. For example, if you look back on your day yesterday, and you see that you got nothing accomplished, or let's say nothing that you feel accomplished about, it's easy to come up with a myriad of excuses as to why, such as: the phone never stopped ringing; I was bothered all day by so-and-so; I had to run a lot of errands, etc. When you look back at those excuses and say nothing got accomplished because of this and that, well, that was your intention.

We always have choices to consider in life. You may not have purposefully and thoughtfully designed your day to play out the way that it did, but, I'd also submit, you probably did not have a well-defined, clear-cut intention to complete the things that would really make you feel that sense of accomplishment. Every moment, you are making choices. You choose not to plan. You choose not to put forethought into how to handle the obstacles that do arise.

When you show up late to an event, you can say it was due to a traffic jam, but the truth is that it was not your clear-cut intention to be on time. We all know about traffic. And we all know if there were 10 million dollars at stake, you would have intended to be there early enough to get your share; you would have made it happen.

If you will take a little time now, write down on paper what your intention is, whether it's your intention for the hour, the day, the week, the month, the year, or your whole life. When you write it down, you can clearly see what your priority is.

Will you stick to that priority? It depends on your real intention.

If you set out to accomplish something during the day, but instead you choose to keep picking up your phone, checking your email, or talking to so-and-so who keeps swinging by your office, at the end of the day, whatever your results were, that was your intention. Your intention was to pick up your phone, check your email, and talk to so-and-so. But, when you are clear about your intention, you choose to be proactive about implementing your mission, so the things that most people are distracted by don't get in your way.

You allow your voicemail to answer your calls. You structure specific time in your day to check emails. You let people know not to disturb you for a certain amount of time. You carve out time to do what you intend to accomplish, and you manifest your intention.

What if you don't know how to manifest your intention? You will work on the small things that you intend to get done, like your daily task list. But what about the major intentions you have that you really don't know how to manifest? What will you DO about your highest intentions?

In some cases, you may not know right away. Often, however, you will know at least one step you can take, and Simply take that first step — even if that first step is just to write it down.

There is usually always some resource available to you that can tell you what the next thing is to do. It may be a person who has done that thing before. It's perfectly acceptable to make an inquiry of people who have been there and done that. A life coach could be an asset to help point you in the right direction. Listening to your intuition, of course, will also play a big role.

But keep in mind, the intention is just the intention. It's what you intend. You do not have to know the exact way just yet. Yes, at some point there will be an action to take, and that is going to be discussed in the next chapter; but what happens often times with so many people is that they feel they have to have the "how" already figured out before they are willing to intend something or commit to it. The reality is that once you "intend", you set the wheels in motion for the "how."

To illustrate this point, I'll refer to one of my favorite quotes on commitment.

Until one is committed, there is hesitancy, the chance to draw back — concerning all acts of initiative (and creation), there is one elementary truth that ignorance of which kills countless ideas and splendid plans: that the moment one definitely commits oneself, then Providence moves too. All sorts of things occur to help one that would never otherwise have occurred. A whole stream of events issues from the decision, raising in one's favor all manner of unforeseen incidents and meetings and material assistance, which no man could have dreamed would have come his way. Whatever

*you can do, or dream you can
do, begin it. Boldness has
genius, power, and magic in it.
Begin it now.*

-Johann Wolfgang von Goethe

When you're first starting to build this new intention-setting skill (habit), it's important not to try to take on too much too soon. Sure, it's easy to get excited about turning over a new leaf, but it's essential that you start where you are NOW, not where you think you SHOULD be.

Setting and manifesting intention takes confidence. You build your confidence through the experience of doing. Set your intentions to do those things you already know how to do and carry them out to completion. Then, when you're comfortable doing what you say you'll do, you can begin to stretch your intention muscles a little more. Only after you get comfortable with the intention-setting process should you start striving for things that might now seem impossible to you.

Be patient with yourself. Take small, measurable steps and keep yourself moving forward. It's very similar to what I suggest when people start working with the Law of Attraction. If you haven't been able to figure out a way to manifest being able to pay the rent every month on time (which is a basic, straightforward, and logical plan of action), how will you manifest a million dollars in the next 90 days? You first have to get good at the basics: keep your word with yourself, do what you say you're going to do, and build your confidence by consistently completing the small daily tasks; then you can take on the more challenging tasks that require a more sophisticated level of manifestation.

Chapter 13: Take Action

Acting is a key point that many personal development gurus leave out! It is necessary to be prepared to take some action. However, the action that you take will not be strenuous or laborious; it will be enjoyable and feel right to you.

Your desires will almost always come through some form of action and through connection to other people. Each of us here on this planet plays a role in the complete operation of the Universe.

You may be familiar with the notion that your thoughts have the power to completely change your life and circumstances. Many of the popular spiritual and new age books and movies out on the market today talk about how to change your thinking so that you can change your life.

While it is true that everything begins with a thought (even you began as a thought in someone's mind!) it takes deliberate action to bring it to fruition.

Your mother could have sat on her couch and meditated until the cows came home about how badly she wanted a baby. But, if she didn't act and make love to your father, you wouldn't be here.

Thomas Edison sat in his workshop and thought about how to manifest the light bulb. He thought, and he thought, and he thought. He believed. He desired. He had faith. But, unless he used his physical hands to experiment in the 10,000 different ways that he experimented with it, he would not have been able to bring about that light bulb.

I don't mean to say that in every case you have to use your bare hands to manifest something. If you have the resources and the communication skills, you can hire people who have the necessary resources to bring about what you want to manifest. That's still an action on your part. You're taking the action of communicating your idea to another soul. You're taking the action of putting money behind it.

Thoughts themselves do not manifest. At the same time, acting without putting any thinking or feeling behind it is every bit as unproductive as having a great idea and not acting on it. Inspired thought and action are both essential ingredients. When your burning desire and all your emotion backs your thoughts, they become an unstoppable force that will carry you to wherever you want to go in life. If you're having trouble acting on your thoughts, you need to get in touch with your "why".

People are motivated by benefits. Until you can clearly see the benefits that come to you by taking action and understand that they far outweigh any benefits that come from lack of action, you may not move.

You see, you are getting some benefits right now out from not taking any action. I could guess what they are, although it can be different for everyone. Essentially, you are getting the benefit of being in your comfort zone. You are getting the benefit of succeeding at something you already do know how to do and avoiding the fear of failing at something you may not know how to do.

If you were to really think about it, you could probably come up with 10 or 100 reasons not to act, and they may be perfectly legitimate. You can justify why you don't move all day long. You've been doing a pretty good job of that up to this point, though you may not really be aware of it. But what about the benefits you would derive by acting on your deepest desires, such as realizing your dreams and goals? What if you knew you could not fail? Would you go for it? What would you have? How would your life be different?

There are only a couple of reasons you would not act.

1. The thing you say you want is not really going to provide you any more positive benefits than what you are getting out of not doing it. If that is the case, then you don't have the right goal.

2. You don't really believe you can have it. If that is the case, why bother? Why bother having a dream if you don't believe you can manifest it? You can't really commit unless you really believe.

How do you acquire enough of that belief in yourself to make you act? By believing. By having faith. By accomplishing one small step at a time. By never giving up. There's only one sure way to succeed, and that is to never, ever give up.

You see, you can do anything — anything you can think of. You were not meant to have dreams that were impossible to manifest. What a cruel joke that would be! You want your belief to come from knowing the exact path, but that is more than likely never going to be available to you as an exact science. Life happens. Change happens. The path you take changes directions.

You see this in everything. You may want to drive across the United States, beginning in Southern California and ending up in Maine. In this case, you do have a pretty clear-cut path to take. But there will likely be roadwork along the way, and you may have to take a detour. It doesn't mean you won't reach your destination. It just means you go as far as you know how to go, and then you work your way around the roadblocks as best you can. Eventually you will get there.

Sometimes this happens when people are trying to lose weight. They have a goal that they want to achieve. Some weeks they lose weight, some weeks they don't. Sometimes they gain weight. But, as long as they continue doing what they know they need to do, like burning more calories than they consume overall, they'll get to their goal.

If you want to start a business on the Internet, you at least know enough that you need a domain name. You start with that. Then you get hosting and put some content on your site. You create your offer, whether it is a service, a product, or being an affiliate of someone else's product. Then you figure out how to attract visitors and get them to become your customer. These are all action steps. There will be smaller action steps in between the bigger ones that you will discover along the way. Some of your actions will take you closer to your goal, and some will take you further away from your goal. But if you keep your intention clear, never give up, consistently act, and have faith that you will succeed, there's no way you can fail.

Maybe you have an idea for an invention. The first thing you're going to want to do is get information on how the process works. Maybe there are books you can read on the topic. Maybe there are consultants you can hire to give you advice on how to proceed. The point is that there is a first step for everything. Luck with anything requires your willingness to take steps towards your desires when those steps are presented to you.

Thinking and believing that you will accomplish a goal will bring about an assortment of opportunities to your awareness, but if you sit at home all day and do not venture out to act at some point, then you're not going to be any closer to achieving that goal.

When you have your intention set that you are going to achieve a goal and you make that commitment to do it, you begin to find clues within your awareness to act upon. This is the way the universe steps in to help you. It's best to accept that invitation from the universe, investigate those clues, and act upon them immediately.

Chapter 14: Other Tips for Creating Good Luck

Practicing Generosity

Now I want you to think about generosity and what it has to do with you becoming a lucky person. Think about how you associate with the people you meet. There will be many people who come into your life, and you will form friendships with some of them.

I would like you to imagine that you are one of those people for a moment — someone who knows you, who has experienced what it is to know you. Just think of the first person that comes to your mind and begin describing yourself from their perception. What do they think about you? What do they feel about you? Do you feel like they like you? Do you think they are inspired to help you in some way? Do they feel motivated to give you insights and information that would help you to grow and prosper and to become lucky in all sorts of ways?

Be honest with yourself and think about those relationships. What are your conversations usually about? Are they one-sided conversations? Are you always looking for a way to turn the conversation into a topic about you? Are you trying to tell them how important or intelligent you are?

Be as clear and true to how others see you as you possibly can. What sense do you get of yourself when you are looking at yourself through different eyes? Another person's point of view can be a real eye opener. Do you like what you are seeing and feeling? Do you come across as a generous person? Is that how someone would describe you? Are you a good friend? In other words, do you listen and care about what other people have to say?

If your answer is no to these questions, then you have the power to change their perceptions of you. No matter where you felt your level of generosity is, you can increase your luck now by becoming a person who is genuinely generous.

Here is how:

Think hard about the word "genuine" and let it sink into your core. Let it awaken your genuinely caring soul — not because it will bring you luck, but because you genuinely desire to have that impact on people.

There is a part of you — you can call it your soul, your spirit, or whatever you want to call it — that is so kind, loving, open, and generous that it is bursting to shine out of you. It is the part of you that consistently looks for ways to make other people happy. You may not have connected to it for a while because you have been preoccupied with your own life. It is hard to feel genuinely considerate and caring towards others when you have been wrestling with your own life and striving for some luck to come your way.

Now, to attract luck into your life, you must embrace your ability to make other people happy. Once you leave a positive impression in someone else's mind, they instinctively have the feeling that they somehow would like to return the gift. That thought alone is warming and fulfilling, and you have created an opportunity for yourself to attract more luck into your life through the generosity of others. Giving makes the event of receiving more likely. Deep down you want to listen to others and have genuine concern and compassion for others. It makes you feel good inside to be this way and know that you are thought of in this way by others.

You have a huge opportunity to be warm and nurturing to someone. You can completely forget about yourself and your needs and pay attention to others. This brings you out of yourself and your own stress and creates something entirely different for others to perceive. They do not see someone who is unlucky and wrapped up in their own affairs, too busy to listen to others. They see someone who is considerate, caring, and compassionate — someone who is strong, willing to be their rock, and who feels that their problems or concerns are completely worthy of your time and attention. Just imagine your friends having that perception of you and how empowering that feels!

The secret to achieving this state is simple. Just let go of your need to impress them at all. All you must do is to listen to them, understand them, and make them feel important. When they feel important to you, you become important to them. Someone who is seen as important is more likely to attract opportunities for themselves.

The only generosity that attracts luck to you is true generosity that comes from your spirit. You cannot attract luck if that is all that motivates you to be generous. To attract luck, you set your true spirit free and allow natural inclinations to guide your actions. You are already generous and giving, I'm sure, in so many ways. But now, you are getting more in touch with the real you who is generous, truly, and it is attractive to others who meet you.

People will sense your powerful and attractive humanitarian nature. Your generosity will be equally extended, even to those you don't know. It is not surprising that most of the good fortune that you will create for yourself will come from people that you don't know. Your new generous approach is that much more impressive and inspiring to someone who does not know you. It defines you as someone who is open and caring and gives without any kind of judgment or reservation. You are far more likely to bring out the generous side of others if you are generous to them first.

From this point on, I want you to work a little harder to understand the problems of your friends and everyone else you meet. Give them assistance without looking for anything in return. Enjoy entering their happiness and feeling like a true and caring friend to them. Enjoy the satisfaction you will feel around you as you see their perception of you change. You may just find yourself becoming one of their closest, truest friends.

As a natural result of your generous and loving ways, you build up a natural positive force all around you. You become surrounded by an abundant reservoir of potential luck that draws in many more opportunities that can be transformed into luck. Your ability to attract luck into your life becomes a natural and growing part of that which you really are, as you grasp hold of a concept that you thought was beyond your reach.

People will now start to get a sense about you that you truly are a friendly person. They will admire your carefree and giving nature. They will be positive around you and give you positive feedback and encouragement in exchange for your generous nature. You make people feel good when they are around you by making them feel important and understood. Just think, every time you exhibit true friendship toward another person, you increase your luck potential.

But the most important lesson here is that you are not doing this just because you want to increase the luck in your life. You are doing this because you are naturally inclined to. Deep down, you truly want to be a better friend, a better person. Everyone does, but they do not always know how to release their generosity and be the best friend they can be.

Listen to your friends. Understand them and be there for them. It is no more complex than that. You can change, but are you also willing? Are you ready to feel the benefits of being a generous, thoughtful, and compassionate friend?

There is no way for you to fool the universe and act generous toward others, expecting some sort of reward in the end, if you're not really feeling it. But if you will simply seek to fulfill your true innate desire to make other people feel good, if you will wish others well and wish them to be successful in all aspects of their life as well, you will be rewarded. Even if you fear that their success might ultimately challenge your success, realize this: true success comes from your ability to move away from the competitive role and toward the creative and/or collaborative role. The universe is abundant. There is no lack of ideas or resources by which to fulfill those ideas. Therefore, the act of helping another person succeed, even where you would like to succeed, does not take away from your potential success. It only enhances the whole of mankind.

Choose to find creative and imaginative ways of improving yourself and becoming a more understanding person. Be a good friend toward others, including those whom you did not know before. The attitude you have toward others is merely a component of the attitude you have toward yourself, so as you make a conscious effort daily to project good positive feelings toward other people and wish them luck in their own lives, you are having this same energy reflected toward you.

Over the next few weeks and months, practice being a better friend to anyone who needs one. In time, you will notice that you have created more lucky opportunities in your life than ever before.

Feng Shui

Feng Shui is an ancient Chinese practice that looks at how things are placed in the environment around you. You can call it your environment since the energies within it directly influence your own. The goal of *Feng Shui* is to finely tune the placement of items, objects, colors, scents and other energy conduits within areas of your environment. This is done to accentuate the auspicious areas and minimize the inauspicious areas. These changes aim to correct the flow of energy or chi that exists in you and in everything.

What you will come to accept is that the laws of the universe affecting heaven and earth can affect a person's life both positively and negatively. By practicing the laws of Feng Shui, you are encouraging universal harmony into your life. This will limit the places that bad luck can be nurtured and stored and will keep its path clear so that it passes through your environment. Good luck can be attracted to areas of your home and magnified so your own chi is more likely to attract it to you. The placement of certain items will reduce the interference and blockages in your energy. This will allow energy, and therefore luck, to flow more freely.

Feng Shui is centered on providing you with protection and good luck in your life. You can use various techniques to overcome bad luck. I will take you through some of the more practical ones that will help enhance the energy flow of your environment and enhance your chances of attracting good luck.

Even if you do not quite understand or buy into the theory behind Feng Shui, you'll come to realize that there is a lot of common sense behind many of its approaches. For example, who doesn't feel better after redecorating a room in their house to look fresh and inviting? Just think about how it feels when you de-clutter an area or re-organize one. It lifts you emotionally and sparks creativity to flow while you are in those areas. You feel more positive and optimistic. Of course, conversely, you can find yourself feeling down in the dumps and restrained in an area where clutter has taken over. An untidy area can cause depressed moods, an unhappy outlook, or feeling overwhelmed. Suddenly, you cannot be bothered to do anything, and you fail to see the point in what you do. These relatively small issues can obviously have a huge impact on how lucky you feel and therefore, how lucky you can be.

A few changes to the areas around you can boost your chi and give you positive vibes, and if you release those vibes into the world, you are more likely to receive a boost of good luck in return. You will start with a cleansing of your own body and energy before moving into the environment around you. That way you will be sure to align your chi with the areas around you, which are essentially an extension of you.

The first step is to take a salt-water bath. You can either bathe in the sea by visiting your nearest beach, or you can prepare a salt water bath at home using 'raw salt'. Salt kills bacteria and germs. It heals wounds, battles skin diseases, and removes polluted energy. Wet your head down to your toes. Lie nice and still, close your eyes, and imagine a spot of bright light at your forehead. Encourage that light to flow down toward your toes through each of your chakra points, pushing all the dark energy down and out of your body.

Next, turn your attention to your home and bedroom. There are several things that you can do to unblock the flow of energy, and the more you do, the better your results will be.

Begin by de-cluttering. Do a thorough spring clean, removing cobwebs and reorganizing furniture and belongings to create space and harmony. Take the time to throw away unwanted things, as these are bad energy-hoarders. Try furniture in different areas to see how it feels. Try a fresh coat of paint. Even just one freshly painted wall could make all the difference in the world.

Now you can reenergize the house by burning sandalwood incense and getting a new water fountain. Let lots of air and energy in by opening your windows. This also allows the sun to shine in, warming your space with natural light. But remember to shut all your windows at dusk before it becomes dark again.

Pay attention to detail. Unclog your drains, sinks, and toilet bowls. Fix things that are broken, such as broken drawers, broken doorknobs, broken locks and worn out switches. All these things drain your energy whenever you approach them or need to use them. Clean the stains from floors and walls. Make your windows and mirrors sparkle, and fill your house with buzzing, positive energy, all of which is likely to pull in good luck.

Fill your surroundings with lots of light — darkness tends to create negativity and sadness, which attracts negative influences. Keep light, especially natural light if possible, flooding into your home through windows. Turn lights on, and light up your home with candles. Burning flames diffuse bad energy and the bad luck right along with it.

There are two key aspects of *Feng Shui* that need to be adhered to because they ensure perfect placement when you rearrange items within your environment.

The first is the Bagua *Feng Shui* areas. The *Feng Shui* Bagua is one of the main tools used to analyze the energy of any given space. When translated from Chinese, Bagua literally means eight areas.

The first step in defining your Bagua is to take a compass reading of your home. Each of the eight *Feng Shui* areas has an element, special colors, and life areas associated with it.

The areas and associations are as follows:

- **North** - The *Feng Shui* element is water; the colors are blue and black; the life areas associated with it are career and Path in Life.

- **Northeast** - The *Feng Shui* element is earth; the colors are beige, light yellow, and sand/earth; the life areas are spiritual growth and self-cultivation.

- **East** - The *Feng Shui* element is wood; the colors are brown and green; the life areas are health and family.

- **Southeast** - The *Feng Shui* element is wood; the colors are brown and green; the life areas are money and abundance.

- South - The *Feng Shui* element is fire; the colors are red, orange, purple, pink and bright yellow; the life areas are fame and reputation.

- **Southwest** - The *Feng Shui* element is earth; the colors are beige, light yellow, and sand/earth; the life areas are love and marriage.

- **West** - The *Feng Shui* element is metal; the colors are white and gray; the life areas are creativity and children.

- **Northwest** -The *Feng Shui* element is metal; the colors are white and gray; the life areas are helpful people, blessings, and travel.

This is only a very basic explanation of the colors, elements, and life areas associated with each Bagua area. In order to create balance and vibrant energy in all areas of your home, you would simply introduce the *Feng Shui* elements and colors into that specific area of your home to enhance that life area.

Of course, you can delve as lightly or deeply into this as you want to, and I provide a much deeper understanding of *Feng Shui* in my other book entitled *Feng Shui* Path on my other website: www.fengshuipath.com.

At first, *Feng Shui* seems very difficult and complex to understand, but once you get the hang of it, you can soon adjust your environment and amplify its ability to help you attract luck as well as wealth, good fortune, love, peace, and happiness. A well-balanced and vibrant home is also the perfect sanctuary for your positive and confident outlook on life.

Morning Luck Meditation

This is a very quick meditation to help to prepare you for the day. It's a good idea to begin the day on a positive note to open you up to an awareness of potential lucky situations and to simply feel like you are a lucky person throughout the day. Just repeating these affirmations within the luck meditation daily will bring about a good feeling, which will help you to be more attractive to lucky encounters.

The first thing you will do every morning before getting out of bed is to listen to this quick meditation, and then go on with the rest of the day.

Let's begin by just sitting up in your bed now while you are just waking up … that's right … we're going to use this time to help bring you into an even more alert wakeful state … a beautiful state that you will be able to carry with you throughout the day … so take in a nice, deep, refreshing and cleansing breath … bring it all the way in … and allow that breath to fill you with a new feeling of awareness and excitement … let that breath fill you with wakeful feelings … and feelings of wonder … just keep breathing in and blowing out old tired feelings … you are excited about waking up for the day and getting to find out just what the rest of the day has in store for you … What if today could be that very special day for you, the one day that changed your life in a positive way, forever … what if today was the luckiest day of your life, and you realized that you were the luckiest person in the world.

Breathe in, and as you let the breath out, you notice a sense of excitement that today really could be that day … Today you will have all sorts of choices to make, like you do every day … but you will notice something about all the choices and decisions that you make today, that each and every one of them is filled with luck potential … that's right … it could be something as simple as deciding to take a new direction while you are driving … or stopping at a new grocery store … or saying hello to a person you've never spoken to before … you are so excited to greet the day today because you sense that today, something really wonderful could happen for you …

Today, you just have a very strong sense that when you go out in the world, things are going to go your way … and you are open to all sorts of wonderful new encounters … you have a zest today … a spring in your step … and a smile on your face … you spend today feeling really good … very happy …

You have decided it's just going to be that kind of day … and so as you are continuing to breathe in and wake up for the day … you can get a sense of how beautiful the weather is … and how you will find just the right parking space … you feel so good … so ready for the day … ready for anything … you just know that everything is going to go your way. Everything will turn out exactly as you would want to have it go … you wake up and you are just buzzing with joy about all the things that you get to do that day … you look forward to getting out of bed … you look forward to mingling with other people …

Now, I want you just to imagine something wonderful, anything at all, something so wonderful happening to you today ... maybe you receive an unexpected gift or money in the mail ... maybe you meet someone who can help you in business ... maybe you meet a man or a woman that you want to date ... or someone who will become a very good friend ... maybe lost or gained that extra pound that you have been wanting ... or maybe it's an advancement in your job or a new job ... but whatever it is, there is something special that could happen today ... and so I want you just to think about some special thing now that could happen ... and then allow that feeling to fill you up all the way from your head down to your toes ... and allow these feelings to be there while you repeat these next affirmations with me ... hear yourself saying them in your own head, loud and clear and with this feeling of joy ...

Today will be filled with all sorts of lucky opportunities.

I am a lucky person.

I experience luck in my life daily.

I am learning how to create more luck.

I attract good fortune.

My intuition is increasing and guiding me toward luck.

I feel my luck is changing for the better.

I am in the right place at the right time.

I enjoy new encounters, which increases my chances of luck.

Today could be the luckiest day of my life.

Good … and now, I want you to think of a lucky affirmation that is personal to you … and I'll give you a moment to repeat that at least three times now … And in a moment I am going to have you open your eyes and when you do … allow them to open up slowly, while at the same time feeling your lips forming a gentle smile … a smile that comes from deep inside your heart … or a place in you that really knows that everything I have said is true and that you will experience a wonderful and lucky day …

As I count from one to three … you'll allow your eyes to slowly open and open a little more with each count … you'll take in a nice, deep, refreshing breath, and your lips will curve to make a beautiful smile and you will be ready to greet the day with a positive, luck-charged attitude … #1 … eyes beginning to open … and lips just barely forming into that smile … #2 … eyes open just a little bit more … and almost a full smile is formed and #3 … open your eyes all the way … and hold that smile while you reach your arms way up high to try to touch the ceiling, and you are all ready now to greet this incredible day, feeling refreshed, alert, awake … and very open and receptive to all the luck that is coming your way today …

Luck Charms

There are so many variations of luck charms that it would be impossible to cover them all here. It is the essence of a good luck charm that is important. They are vessels of hope, courage, and protection because the wearer has deemed them as such.

Your desire to have something to safeguard those qualities that you feel are illusive is not uncommon. Luck charms are a symbol of the fact that you believe in luck. If you have ever found yourself possessing or wearing a lucky charm, then clearly, at least some part of you believes that you do have some influence over your luck. This is a powerful feeling that can change your approach to a situation.

You carry yourself with an inner faith. Your confidence gets a boost. Your frame of mind is set to achieve, to take on greater challenges, and to put your very best into a situation. For many people these charms are an anchor of strength that reminds them that luck is on their side if they will it to be.

Lucky charms have been around for centuries. It is hard to deny their power and effectiveness when so many people refuse to be parted from the ones they have acquired. How many times have you heard someone say, "Oh, wait a minute, I need my good luck charm?" Or it may sound more like, "Wait, I need my lucky socks, or my lucky coin, or, my lucky pendent." The array of items that people empower as being lucky is astonishing. I've heard of lucky rocks, lucky rabbit's feet, and lucky numbers. Can all of these objects really be "lucky"? Can you prove they are not?

A good luck charm is an object that creates a positive influence over the fortunes of the person that possesses it. It is believed that certain objects have the power to emit positive or negative spiritual energy. The real magic for many, however, takes place in the mind. Tests have shown that people genuinely feel luckier while wearing a good luck charm. You may feel more daring and more eager to take advantage of those opportunities that come your way. This in and of itself increases the chances of being lucky.

Those types of good luck charms tend to rely on the power of suggestion and are symbolic in nature. Other kinds of charms, such as Vedic Talismans, bring good luck to the wearer through a combination of positive spiritual energy produced from their physical form, the spiritual energy that is absorbed during their blessing, and through the faith placed in them by those who own them. Both types of charms are powered by the faith their users place in them.

Once the positive spiritual energy of a lucky object has been recognized, it can release its potential to bring about good. Lucky objects can also be used to ward off the negative effects of bad periods and enhance the positive ones. You may carry around this lucky catalyst to help influence a situation simply by having it with you. If you like, you can consider it your anchor. Just knowing it is there, makes you feel confident that you will attract good luck.

So what kind of lucky charm will serve you best? There are certainly plenty out there that could give you the boost you need each day.

Think of an amulet, however, as a physical extension of all the luck you possess. It cannot give you good luck all by itself. You must believe in luck, and you must believe you can be lucky. You believe that something about this object contains the ability for you to tap into luck. By holding it, looking at it, wearing it ... or however you tap into it, it can help you believe in yourself. Once you have worn it or used it the first time and felt luckier with it on that self-belief, the power of the amulet grows stronger.

There are many good luck charms that you will no doubt have heard of. I am sure you are familiar with the four-leaf clover and the luck of the Irish, as well as the horseshoe, the rabbit's foot, feathers, stones and coins. Natural stones or pebbles contain earth energy, making them a desirable good luck charm. Specifically, quartz, agate, and jade are considered lucky gemstones.

As I said before, once you have called something your good luck charm, that is what it becomes. It can be unique, specific, and personal to you. It brings luck to you, but possibly to no one else — unless of course, you bestow that lucky object onto another, and they feel the luck that it carries.

There is also something powerful about the universal understanding of the many charms that are popular throughout the world's different cultures.

Some of the many examples of these are listed below:

Tigers are considered lucky in Chinese astrology. The tiger is also considered a protector against certain evils, including theft and fire.

The Rabbit's Foot is a popular charm, carried for good luck and protection. Because of the rabbit's reputation in procreation, it is said to enhance the wearer's chances of becoming a parent.

A Buddha charm or statue is thought of as being lucky, especially if you rub Buddha's belly. It symbolizes enlightenment and the journey to a truly content and happy future.

Dream catchers originated in Native America and are considered good fortune because they catch negative images from dreams. They are also thought to ward off bad dreams, keeping your thoughts sunny and pure while you sleep.

Horseshoes are believed to bring good fortune when they are hung up on the wall of a home or above a doorway. Even the blacksmiths who made horseshoes were lucky. Horseshoes symbolize the strength and dependability of the horse. The horseshoe is said to protect your house and land.

The Number Seven is widely recognized as lucky, throughout the world. There are a few cultures that hold the number in high esteem, including the U.S. It is also important in some of the major world religions including Buddhism, Hinduism, and Christianity.

The four-leaf clover, or shamrock, is said to give you the luck of the Irish. Four leaf clovers do exist, but they are far less common than the three-leaf variety. Therefore, finding one is said to be good luck. Legend has it that when Eve had to leave paradise, she took a four-leaf clover along for good luck. It seems she took a little bit of paradise with her, so all four-leaf clovers connect back to Eden.

Bamboo is considered good luck, particularly in China, and specifically the Dracaena (druh-see-nuh) Sanderiana, which is the botanical name for "Lucky Bamboo." It is a member of the lily family that grows in the tropical rainforests of Southeast Asia and Africa. It needs little attention to survive, making it a very durable and life loving plant.

The lucky penny will always have people reaching down to pick it up. If it is laying heads up, then it is supposed to be lucky. The luck of a coin is always enhanced when there is a bend, a hole, or a scrape on it that makes it unique. The luck of such coins is enhanced if they are worn around the neck or carried in a left-hand pocket.

Coins in general are very versatile good luck charms. A jar of pennies kept in the kitchen can bring you luck. A coin in a new jacket, handbag, purse, or wallet will also bring good luck. A coin as a good luck charm is supposed to attract more good luck to it. Some also believe that a coin minted in a leap year will bring good fortune.

A shark's tooth is said to have protective and healing powers in addition to bringing good luck. Many people wear them on necklaces or keep them somewhere in their house.

The cross is a well-known Christian symbol said to ward off evil and protect the person who wears it. Legend has it that the undead cannot attack you if you hold up a cross — the symbol of God — as good deflects evil.

The gemstone amber is thought to be a piece of the sun with the power to bring good fortune. The Greeks called this amber "electron", which gave us our word electricity. It gives off sparks when rubbed, making it appear to be a source of energy.

The sapphire is an ancient symbol of good luck. The Greeks believed that to wear it was to invite the favor of the gods. In the Middle East, it is believed to have supernatural powers. In India it is believed to have the power to bring health and wealth. It is thought to repel dangers and protect the purity of the wearer.

The Cat's Eye keeps the path ahead of you clear. It is believed to remove obstacles and help you to move ahead in life, and to ward off negative planetary influences, ghosts, and spirits. It is also said to protect you from unforeseen losses in business and in your career. It helps to ensure financial stability by guarding your wealth.

How does a luck charm come about for you? You might make a lucky charm, or you could purchase one. You may even simply find one. We've all been compelled to pick up that penny lying on the street or smile when we come across a four-leaf clover. Our attraction to good luck charms runs deep and is a powerful aspect of society in all cultures. Your choice of charm will be easy because you will know and covet it as lucky the moment you set eyes on it.

White Magic Luck Spells

White Magic generally applies to healing and helping magic spells. It is the magic of good.

Whether you are a believer or not, the spell below can be applied with ease and will focus your mind on attracting luck to you.

Tools: Paper and pen

Ritual: Prepare your work area by laying out the objects you would use on a normal day. Have the paper and pen close to hand.

From the very start of this process, you will **think about your intention.** See what you desire in your mind and know what it is you are aiming for. Do not let negative thoughts enter your mind. Concentrate on your goal.

Draw a circle in the air around your workspace using your index finger. Imagine it glowing — a light blue ray of light circling your area of creativity.

As you imagine that circle in the center of the space out in front of you, see the thick line becoming thicker until it **forms a sphere of light blue energy** in the center of your work area. **Concentrate on that sphere of light.**

Close your eyes and direct all your energy into that sphere.

Open your eyes and let the sphere float before you. Keep it still and central.

Now, take your pen and paper and write down what it is you want to bring about.

Fold the paper four times and then hold it out so that your hand and the paper enter the sphere of light.

As you do this, **say:** "This sphere represents the good luck that will manifest my intention."

Let the sphere grow so that it surrounds you and your workspace, then place the paper in the center of the circle.

Say, "As the paper absorbs the light, I shall absorb the good luck I seek."

Sit back and **imagine the light grow smaller** and sink into the paper in front of you.

Envision what you will look and feel like when you have the luck contained. See yourself holding the object you desire or with the desired goal you wish to achieve. See yourself when your good luck arrives.

Say, "As the blue light dissipates with time, good luck will be mine."

Continue to meditate as the light vanishes.

Take the piece of paper and rip it up into small pieces.

Repeat the affirmation: "As the blue light dissipates with time, good luck will be mine."

Sweep the pieces of paper away and sprinkle them into the earth so they can mix with nature's power and summon good luck into your life.

Chapter 15: Luck in Specific Areas of Your Life

Luck with Money

You attract money by making money. How many times have you heard that? Of course, there is some truth in it. You attract good luck to your finances by being in the process of obtaining money, pursuing work that you are passionate about, being responsible with your savings, and keeping a positive search for further fortunes ongoing. As you continue seeking out new opportunities, you keep the faith and the belief in your ability to make money and keep some saved for a rainy day.

Each of those components is just as important as the other. If you have some money saved, you feel far more financially secure. Imagine what would happen if your car broke down, or your pet or your child became sick, or you had disaster in your home. What would you do? If you were unlucky, you would have no money saved, and you would see it yet another instance of misfortune, just another horrible event that compounds the fact that your life is not destined to get any easier.

Instead of feeling that luck has got it in for you and that the moment you start to relax something awful happens, what if you had a safety net? What if, instead, you had prepared for the unexpected and felt lucky because you had put a little money aside in a savings account? Your attitude would be entirely different. You would be saying things like, "Thank goodness it was nothing too serious," or, "I'm lucky I had money set aside just in case," or, "Well, at least I was prepared." That little bit of money turned the unexpected into something manageable instead of something disastrous. The lucky-minded individual survives surprises because they look for and create the positives in their circumstances.

There are many ways you can look for opportunities that will help you attract money. Sometimes this might mean taking calculated risks, trying something new and potentially rewarding. You may not feel like the kind of person who can break out of their comfort zone, but honestly, that is where the money is. It is certainly not in what you are doing now, if you are looking for ways to make money. You could settle for doing what you are doing forever, or you could try a change in direction. Not every change is a good one, but A) you learn from your failures and your experiences, and B) when the right opportunity does come along, you need to be able to act for that right opportunity to be lucky.

It takes some courage to act and to reach that next level of good fortune. You must be willing to do something different than what the norm tells you to do, because, let's face it, the norm is not wealthy. The only thing that really sets you apart from the norm is how you think. If you think you are lucky with money, you will fulfill that prophesy. Nothing is stopping you from being one of those lucky people. Nothing at all, except that you've been listening to the part of your brain that is telling you it doesn't happen for people like you. But why not you?

Just because it hasn't happened yet, doesn't mean it isn't going to. There are many small changes you can make that will drive you towards good luck and attract it to you in return. Do you think that your job is the only thing keeping you from making money? These days, there are many ways to make money through the Internet if you will only take some time to get creative, investigate, and think outside the box. If you intend to make a certain level of wealth, you can allow fresh ideas to come to you. It doesn't have to be the ways in which you know. Ways in which you may have not thought about before will appear to you, once you start to open your mind to new ideas.

Be proactive with the money you do have and invest it wisely. Really think about what you spend your money on. Are you spending your money frivolously and foolishly on things that only bring you temporary satisfaction? Spending your money mindlessly shows a lack of respect for money, for yourself, and for the time and energy that go into earning that money.

Instead, spend your money in ways that will make you happy and healthy and that invest in who you are becoming, such that you can sustain your ability to create even more money. All you need to add is self-belief. Bless the money you spend, even when you must pay bills or taxes. Be grateful that you have the money to make your house warm and that you make enough money to be in your tax bracket.

When you see people who have wealth, don't be jealous or envious or make assumptions about their integrity. Imagine what it has taken for them to get to that place. If you choose to call them "lucky bastards" you are giving luck — the luck you are trying to achieve — a bad association in your own mind. But when you look upon them with admiration, awe, and curiosity, your brain does something different. It seeks to understand how you can attain such a wonderful thing. Know that you can make more money and decide that you will. Do not look for the proof that it hasn't worked and assume it's time to throw in the towel. Instead, seek for proof that you can do it!.

If you are feeling that you are stuck in a rut or that you are just predestined to be hard up, we call that a bad luck magnet. If you ooze those kinds of negative emotions around business deals, then you are screaming, "I am a bad investment, take your money elsewhere." You must radiate financial buoyancy and positivity right where you stand in order to attract a little luck your way. Those who look secure and content look like safe investments. When you come across as strong, people believe you are a safe bet. This will attract those who want to invest in you, whether it be through a partnership, giving you a position in their company, or investing money in you or an idea that you have.

You can feel wealthy and act wealthy, even if you don't have millions in your bank account. If you look at all the things in your life money cannot buy, it gives you that sense of gratitude, which gives you a sense of being lucky. The luckier you feel, the luckier you become.

Julia Cameron summed up what being lucky with money feels like when she said, "What we really want to do is what we are really meant to do. When we do what we are meant to do, money comes to us, doors open for us, we feel useful, and the work we do feels like play to us."

To be lucky with money, find out what you love. What were you put on this Earth to do? What is your calling? If you can find that, you will find your fortune. It will not be the money that completes you; it will be doing what you love every day. And that is priceless.

For more information about Learning to Attract Money, www.fengshuipath.com

Luck with Love

Is your goal to find "the one"? Do you think you can you be lucky in love?

Then put some effort into getting out there and meeting people. How else will people find you if you are not making yourself known? You have the power to create opportunities so that luck can be attracted into your love life. Luck can only happen when your actions are in alignment with your desires.

The opportunity might be something like getting a phone number or being invited out by a friend who brings along someone you have been gazing at from afar. The times you try to talk to someone who is not interested are just steps toward finding the one who is interested.

You are not unlucky if you get turned down or are simply not compatible with someone. You are just in a situation that you can learn from and then refine your search. Each time you accept a rejection you are moving closer to getting lucky and finding the right partner for you.

If you desire to be lucky in love, approach the world as love being open to love. Let people know that you are single and happily in search for someone special. Go out into the world each day and embrace every opportunity to meet people. You never know exactly where each conversation could lead. As you open yourself up even a little bit, potential partners have an easier time seeing the love in you that you have to offer and will be attracted to you the more you are open to sharing that love.

The next time someone asks you if you are single, you say, "Yes, I am," and then, "Do you know anyone great that I should meet?" Smile boldly and be content with who you are. Expand your horizons. Be open to giving the unknown a try; you just never know what you may be missing out on when you say "no" to people about whom you make assumptions or judgments.

Be persistent. It does take energy to keep your search for love going until you have found it. It really is all up to you at the end of the day. Use your network of friends to create more links for you to try. Get involved in big social gatherings where you can see new faces and socialize as much as you can.

Finally, love yourself. Believe in yourself. Do not let fears and excuses keep you from receiving love. People in love come in all shapes and sizes. Every single relationship is different than the next; different outlooks, different passions and interests, different abilities, different likes and dislikes, etc. Your relationship, if that is what you are looking for, simply has not been made yet. But know this: one thing you can be sure of is that if you want a love relationship, if you stay persistent, luck in love will find you.

Here are a few practical ways that you can look for love if you are determined to find it:

Keep your appearance fresh and sharp. Change something — get a new hairstyle or even update your wardrobe. Always be well-dressed and ready to meet someone. You never know whom you might bump into, even in the grocery store, the bookstore, or the coffee shop.

Stay current and well-informed on topics that interest you, so you have plenty to talk about when you do meet someone or strike up a conversation with people in social settings.

Say yes. Say yes when your friends invite you out. Say yes to holidays. Say yes to anything fun (and legal, of course)! You are more likely to meet people when you are out with your friends or doing things you really enjoy, because you are being your true and likeable self. Your true colors come out, and that stands out to potential new love interests. Your genuine self is your best self.

Do not be shy. Life is short. Take the plunge and go introduce yourself. If they are not interested in you, accept it graciously, as it only gets you one step closer to someone who is. And what if they do turn out to be interested? You'll never know unless you try.

And finally, **be honest.** Do not try to be something or someone you are not, because plenty of people will love you for exactly the person you already are.

For more information about Learning to Attract Your Soulmate, visit:

www.SoulmateAttractionKit.com

Luck with Health

There has been endless debate over whether someone who is ill can "think them self better" with a positive attitude. We've all experienced that feeling of dread when a cold is coming on. What you do with that information can make all the difference in your life. You can say something like, "Oh, I'm feeling a little run down. I know it's just temporary. I'll just take a quick break and be as good as new." Or you can say, "Oh no, I guess I'm going to get sick. I always get sick. It always lasts so long. Why do I always catch a cold?" and then suffer with a cold for the next one to two weeks. Our mental attitude has a huge impact on how we feel, emotionally as well as physically.

To be positive and hopeful while ill is far more nurturing than to succumb to feeling rotten. Of course, the more positive you feel about yourself, the more likely you are to simply take great care of yourself in the first place.

If you feel depressed or have a bad day, how do you handle that? Do you strive to match up your outer conditions with how you are feeling on the inside? Are you likely to eat for comfort, skip the gym, and curl up on the sofa watching TV? Or do you look for ways to balance out the bad with the good. A positive, energetic person knows that going to the gym will give them a wonderful endorphin rush, and they'll feel much better about themselves. They'll nurture themselves with a healthy meal, read an uplifting book, meditate, or do hypnosis and get a good night's sleep.

When you put emphasis on feeling good and creating good health you always feel as though you deserve to feel good about yourself, and therefore you are kinder to your body, especially when you feel as though you were beat up.

It is your approach to life that matters. A terminal illness can take away your outer shell, but your inner mind can fight to be true to itself until the very end. Know who you are and how you wish to be seen. That is the person that luck will visit. That is the person more likely to pull through because they have plans, and they see themselves as more than just a physical body.

The most nurturing combination for your health is to expect good fortune. Good feelings have a positive impact on the body. Expecting to feel bad, expecting to die, and living in fear all create negative feelings in the body and have a negative impact. Maximize your chances of something good happening by seizing upon opportunities, listening to your impulses, coping with bad luck by learning from it, and continuing to live in the gratitude of all that you do still have.

You can be grateful for food that heals and nourishes your body. You can be grateful for having family members and friends who care for you. You can be grateful for the parts of your body that are healthy and for the ability to read or listen to this book, which could lead you toward the very road you need to be on to become healed. You can be grateful for all the many wonderful years you have been on this planet and experiences you have already had and for the doctors who are concerned and compassionate toward you. There are so many things to be grateful for when that is where you put your focus. I beat this drum of gratitude because it is one of the highest positive vibrations you carry, and it can certainly be a catalyst in your healing.

How you approach your health when you are in relatively good health already is important to mention here as well. Genetics do play a role in our health and in our bodies, no question. But if your intention is to have a slender or well-defined body you can create that. The energy and persistence you put in at the gym, or into an active lifestyle, as well as your nutritionally balanced diet, will be the main contributing factor to your body's physical appearance. Your positive outlook on life will keep your mind and your body healthy as you continue to focus on your good luck in all areas of your life. Even your posture will be straighter because when you have more confidence, you walk with your chin held high. You look beyond illness by focusing on the health you want, not on the ill health you don't want.

If you are dealing with pain in the body, stop complaining about it to everyone you know. Just stop giving it so much attention. Put your mind on things you can do to feel good, see yourself as healthy, and commit to living a healthy lifestyle.

You can be lucky in your health and create miracles in your body as a result of thinking of excellent health.

The mind and the body are connected, and if you can surround yourself with thoughts of health, it's bound to make an improvement in the way you feel, even if it's only a little bit. A little bit can be just enough to keep you motivated to see what else you can do toward feeling a little better and little better each day.

Finally, let's close this segment by getting back to the concept of generosity again. Be there for the people who need you. If someone in your life is going through a spell of bad health, reassure them that they have someone supporting them. As you send them your positive well wishes and become the warmth and encouragement they need, you are creating a positive flow of energy toward yourself, because all actions directed toward others ultimately are directed back to you anyway.

Luck with Career

This is perhaps the biggest area for luck to feature in our lives. "Oh, he was lucky, landing that job — is he even qualified?" is just one possible comment someone has uttered about another person. Have you ever exclaimed surprise when someone has told you where they work or about a sale they made or how much money they make? In your head you were screaming, "What? How did she manage that?" You wish them well, but inside you're ridiculing them about their dumb luck, and at the same time, beating yourself up for not being as lucky as they seem to be.

This is a surefire way to repel luck. It comes back to the idea that there's not enough to go around; if someone else gets something, it takes from me. It's the attitude of fear and lack that causes that reaction.

Bottom line: you need to be genuinely happy for others in their career, as if you were happy for yourself. You are then saying, "Ah yes, I see other people are getting great careers, and I'm on the verge of my lucky break too." If I haven't said it enough, I'll say it one more time, we become what we believe.

Are you happy with your career? If you're not satisfied in your career, what about it is unsatisfying? What would your ideal career look like? Do you want more money? More opportunity for advancement? Are you just settling for a job because "we're in a bad economy and this is the best I can do right now?"

Where is your focus? Are you focused on how bad it is? Are you focused on how you keep getting passed over? If this is where you are focused, this is what you will continue to get.

Look past all that. Look at what your ideal career would offer you and take steps toward having that. The key is to get focused on what you want and get on the path toward getting it.

If you discover you aren't even in the right job right now, that doesn't mean quitting your job immediately and pounding the pavement tomorrow. It means being willing to be honest and ask yourself, "Am I happy here?" And if the answer is no, "What would make me happy?" And if you don't know what would make you happy, that is where your path begins. Doing the necessary soul searching to find out what would make you happy.

Does it mean having to go back to school and re-educate yourself in a new field? Does it mean maybe you would prefer self-employment rather than working for a boss? Does it mean deciding that maybe you're not cut out for self-employment and going back to look for a steady career in the same field?

You have a right to be happy doing what you spend most of your waking time doing. Even if heading in a different direction means a temporary sacrifice, if you can handle whatever the sacrifice is, won't you feel like the luckiest person in the world when you are finally making money doing something you absolutely love? Perhaps you are in the right career, but there's just something about it that has been unsatisfying. What can you do to make it better?

It goes back to your thoughts and your perception again. What are you thinking about? What are you focused on? What do you like about your career? What are you grateful for? Even changing just one minor detail about your job can make a huge difference in your attitude. Figure out what is bothering you. You can do only two things with that information. Change it or accept it.

If deep down inside of you, you know there is a golden opportunity waiting for you, then it's time to take that idea to the next level:

As vividly as you can, **imagine all the details** that really matter to you in your perfect career. Be prepared and ready to jump on the opportunities as they are presented to you.

Always maintain a sharp appearance. You never know how or when those opportunities will present themselves. When you enter an interview, you will look as every bit as professional and determined as you come across.

Create a great resume that really stands out from the rest of the crowd. Make it informative but interesting. Good luck is more likely to favor the creative, standout individual than the mundane, generic candidate.

Prepare for interviews and meetings like you were preparing to give a very important speech. You want to make yourself the obvious choice. You want to be so confident in yourself that you are the one with many choices, not the other way around.

If you do have a bad experience at an interview, **think about what you can learn from it.** There is really no such thing as failure, only feedback. Keep moving forward. It may not have worked out this time, but with persistence you will ultimately get exactly what you wanted.

If you missed out on an opportunity, don't sit there and dwell on it as if it was the only opportunity you'll ever have. There are an abundance of opportunities waiting for you, and you are the perfect choice for that one special career. Dust yourself off quickly and look to the next chance. That other one just probably wasn't the right one for you.

The more **guts and sheer determination** you put into attracting the right career, the more you will enhance your good luck. The time and energy will produce the results that you want. Each opportunity is just taking you one step closer and making you that much more polished and readier for opportunities to find you.

Again, we're talking about luck here. **You attract good luck based on the way you think and act upon opportunities.** If you have been working at finding a career for some time, think about how many people you are meeting. Your network of colleagues expands, and more and more people know what you are capable of.

When people ask about your success, replace statements like "Oh, I do ok," and "Well, you can only do your best," with, "I think I do very well," and, "I like to give my best". These are positive statements that will sound direct and confident. Hence, you will feel certain and confident. If you give out insecure vibes, you will feel insecure and experience the bad luck that is a direct result of those kinds of thoughts. If you give out noncommittal statements, you then are showing your lack of certainty within yourself. Be certain of your journey and know your true vocation. Let that clear objective be known by the way you walk, talk, and carry yourself. That clear intention is what makes you stand out as the obvious choice.

How do you like to see yourself in a work environment? Choose to behave as the successful, positive, passionate person you want to be, and luck will follow your clear decision. When you arrive at work, envision a successful and fruitful day ahead of you. Look at what you need to get done and what you do to make a real difference in people's lives. You have an opportunity, no matter what your job is, to stand out. You have an opportunity to inspire people every day. Don't involve yourself with the gossip, as it will only come back to you. Talk positively to colleagues and motivate others when appropriate. That energy will be returned to you as the office will buzz with positive energy.

It is your attitude that will bring about opportunities for you to advance your career. Once those opportunities start to appear, you will feel lucky in your work, and better still, other people will see you as lucky.

Luck with Winning

Never expect to lose. That is the golden rule when aspiring to achieve a winning attitude. That does not mean that you must be arrogant or overly ambitious, but it does mean that you should expect to win.

That attitude will give you the motivation to keep trying, to keep entering competitions, quizzes, and lotteries, even. The fact is that you cannot win anything you are not in!

If you expect to lose, you'll never have the motivation to keep entering, day after day. You will not have the motivation to train for a sports event or the motivation to study for an exam. Imagining your win is what drives you to reach it.

Any kind of competition, challenge, or test relies on your approach to it. If you put in a full effort and believe that you can win, clearly you have more of a chance of winning when that single moment you have been waiting for comes around. If you fear losing and try to cushion your fall by only putting in partial effort, then losing is surely going to be the result.

You must commit to winning if you wish to win. A winning outlook in life is one of persistence, determination, and focus. Lucky people tend to listen to their intuition, which helps them to avoid bad situations and maximize good opportunities. If you have a feeling that you'll win a writing contest, for example, don't let your brain talk you out of entering. It's all too easy to say, "Oh, I'm not good enough to win." Listen to your intuition telling you that you are good enough. You will never really know what is possible unless you try.

You can develop your intuition by taking some quiet time for yourself. Allow yourself time to think and reflect on decisions you have made. Taking a nice, long walk in the woods, or a hot, soaking bath, or having a hobby you can lose yourself in are all good for cleansing the soul. These quiet times reward you for all the positive energy you exert in your life. You need relaxation time to recharge and see your accomplishments through a fresh pair of eyes.

You will automatically go into situations with a stronger sense of what victory feels like. You will be able to see yourself winning what you desire most. Buying a lottery ticket requires the same approach. Imagine yourself winning and keep entering. Remember, you cannot win anything you are not in.

Sometimes winning is a surprise. These moments that are filled with luck come about as a result of energy you have created in other aspects of your life. You always strive to achieve greatness in every role you ever play. You strive to attract luck to you through every situation you engage in. You may not see direct results come about from the energy you put into one specific area, but the fact that you are having an impact on the world around you might just be creating remuneration through winning at some jackpot.

You are always attracting your luck. And sometimes that good luck comes about as a reward for a job well done. Apply these five changes to your life, and you are sure to get more luck than you can handle:

1. Work honestly, knowing that some rewards are not always immediately obvious.

2. Imagine yourself winning anything that you strive for.

3. Enter any challenge, game, or contest that appeals to you, and always try your best in the face of any challenge. The more you enter, the better your chances are of winning.

4. Get a few small wins under your belt so that you feel empowered and lucky when you go for the ones that truly matter.

5. Bounce back from any setback by telling yourself it is not failure — it is just one step towards victory.

Chapter 16: Summary and Conclusion

By now, the word likely buzzing around your brain is opportunity. Opportunities are all around you. That is what you discover as you open your eyes and awaken to the real understanding that you can, and you do attract all the luck (the bad as well as the good) that you have in your life.

You have begun to align your mind with luck. By focusing on what you desire you will create a path towards it. If you do not aim at what you want, how will you ever get to it? Your new positive mental attitude will be empowering, and it will put a smile on your face and a skip in your step. You are in control of your luck. You can overcome bad luck and change your own fortune.

Remember to learn from everything that has happened in your past and then move forward from it. Always be prepared to take new opportunities as they arrive. By staying present, alert, and aware, you notice more opportunities. It is time to take a few chances and reap the rewards.

Above all else, believe in yourself. Know that you are no different than those who have had amazing amounts of luck. You, too, deserve good luck. You deserve to accomplish what you desire to achieve in life. If you believe in yourself, others will believe in you too, leading to more opportunities, new relationships, more career enhancements, better health, wealth, and abundance, and more wins across every aspect of your life.

Remember, you are more powerful than you realize. And I hope you will continue your journey toward a very prosperous, fortunate, luck-filled life from this moment on. Set your intention now to creating good luck and acting. Go back and re-read this book and do your very best to complete all the exercises.

I wish you the very best of luck, but you will not need mine anymore because you will now be making plenty of your own.

About the Author

Victoria Gallagher is a worldwide leader in

Hypnotherapy, a best- selling author, international speaker, life success coach, and renowned authority on the law of attraction.

Since 1999, Victoria has influenced the lives of hundreds of thousands of people. As creator of a

vast library of unique and powerful personal development programs, she helps people change limiting beliefs and achieve their dreams. Her work receives countless high reviews on her popular website Hyptalk.com, which attests to the effectiveness of these programs.

Victoria's work caught the interest of ABC's 20/20 in July 2013, where she was interviewed by Dan Harris in an episode entitled "Got Luck?" She's also been a featured guest on dozens of other radio and online talk shows.

As a tireless personal growth enthusiast herself, Victoria hosts two popular weekly Law of Attraction talk shows, "Law of Attraction Live" and her podcast called "The Power of Your Mind." Both shows feature industry experts and is a powerful platform where you get high value tips and strategies, useful in your everyday life.

Victoria lives an adventurous dream lifestyle in the hiking mecca and scenic town of Cave Creek, Arizona. When she and her soulmate and husband of 10 years, Steve Gallagher, are not busy travelling the world, they spend their free time playing around with their three beautiful housecats, Emerald, Sebastian and Velvet.

You can learn more about Victoria Gallagher at VictoriaMGallagher.com

Free Resources and eBooks by Victoria Gallagher

Law of Attraction Mastery App by Hyptalk:

https://itunes.apple.com/us/app/law-of-attraction-mastery/id895682712?mt=8

Meditation Magnetism eBook Available at:

https://meditationmagnetism.com/ebook

The Empowered Life – eBook Available at:

https://personalgrowthclub.com/empowered

Thoughts to Money – eBook Available at:

https://www.thoughtstomoney.com/thoughtstomoney

Victoria M. Gallagher Website:

http://www.VictoriaMGallagher.com

Made in the USA
Lexington, KY
25 September 2019